D1536624

DAYS OF THE SPIRIT

Volume 1
Advent to Lent

J. MASSYNGBAERDE FORD

A Liturgical Press Book

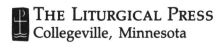

THE LITURGICAL PRESS
Collegeville, Minnesota

Cover design by Greg Becker.

1	2	3	4	5	6	7	8

Library of Congress Cataloging-in-Publication Data

Ford, J. Massyngbaerde (Josephine Massyngbaerde)
    Days of the Spirit / J. Massyngbaerde Ford.
       p.   cm.
    Includes bibliographical references.
    Contents: v. 1. Advent to Lent.
    ISBN 0-8146-2217-8 (v. 1)
    1. Church year meditations. 2. Catholic Church—Prayer-books and devotions—English.   I. Title.
BX2170.C55F56 1994
242'.2—dc20
                                                    93-40551
                                                      CIP

Contents

Third Week of the Year

Fourth Week of the Year

Fifth Week of the Year

Sixth Week of the Year

Acknowledgments

A sincere effort has been made to trace copyright. If any omissions or errors have been made, please let us know so that we may correct them in future editions. We gratefully acknowledge the following sources:

Vicente Aleixandre, "Ciudad del Paraiso;" San Juan de la Cruz, "Cancion de la subida del Monte Carmelo;" Jorge Guillen, "Epifania;" Fray Luis de Leon, "Vida Retirada;" Antonio Machado, "Galerias;" Francisco de Mediano, "Si la voz" Tuso de Molina, "Segadores" Pedro Salinas; from *The Penguin Book of Spanish Verse*, New Parallel Text Edition, 3rd edition, © 1988 by Viking Penguin. Reprint permission requested of Penguin Books.

An Anthology of Spanish Poetry: From the Beginnings to the Present Day, Including Both Spain and Spanish America, edited by John A. Crow, © 1979 by Louisiana State University Press. Reprinted by permission of Louisiana State University Press.

Isaac Felipe Azofeifa, "Poema de la Bomba H con el Proverbio de Una Madre India;" Francisco Luis Bernardez, "El Libertador;" Jorge Luis Borges, "El Hombre;" Ernesto Cardinal, "Salmo 7;" Jose Hierro, "Nino;" Juana de Ibarbourou, "Millonarios;" Gregorio Reynolds, "Ojos;" Miguel de Unamuno, "A la Libertad;" from Manuel Mantero, *Los Derechos del Hombre en la Poesia Hispanica Contemporanea*, Antologia Hispanica, © 1973. Reprint permission requested of Camara del Libro (Spain).

Leonardo Boff, *Los Sacramentos de la Vida*, 8th edition, © 1989 by Coleccion Alcance, 1, Editorial "Sal Terrae," Santander. Reprint permission requested of Coleccion Alcance (Spain).

Francisco Brines, "El por que de las Palabras;" Pureza Canelo, "La Luz;" Miguel Hernandez, "El Nino Yuntero;" Blas de Otero, "Cuerpo de la Mujer;" "Paso a Paso;" Claudio Rodriguez, "Siempre La Claridad Viene del Cielo;" from *Recent Poetry of Spain, a Bilingual Anthology*, translated by L. Hammer and S. Schyfter, © 1983 by Sachem Press. Reprint permission requested of Sachem Press.

Ernesto Cardenal, *Nueva Antologia Poetica*, 7th edition, © 1988 by Siglo Veintiuno Editores (Mexico). Reprinted by permission of Siglo Veintiuno Editores.

Rosario Castellanos, "La Annunciacion;" "La Oracion del Indio;" from *Poesia No Eres Tu*, first reprint, © 1981 by Fondo de Cultura Economica (Mexico). Reprint permission requested of Fondo de Cultura Economica (Mexico).

Sor Juana Ines de la Cruz, *Obras Completas*, "Sepan Cuantos . . . ," Num. 100, © by Editorial Porrua, S. A., Av. Republica Argentina. Reprint permission requested of Editorial Porrua, S. A., Av. Republica Argentina.

Ezequiel Martinez Estrada, "Bienvenida a los Reyes Magos;" Gabriela Mistral, "La Maestra Rural;" from *Antologia de la Poesia Espanola e Hispanoamericana*, edited by F. de Onis, © 1961 by Las Americas Publishing Company. Reprint permission requested of Las Americas Publishing Company.

Carmen Bernos de Gasztold, "The Centipede," translated by Rumer Godden in *Creatures Choir*, © 1965 by Viking Press. Reprint permission requested of Viking Press.

Vicente Huidobro, "Canto IV," from *Altazor, Temblor de Cielo*, 5th edition, edited by R. de Costa, © 1989 by Ediciones Catedra, S. A. (Spain). Reprinted by permission of Ediciones Catedra, S. A. (Spain).

Juana de Ibarbourou, "Carne Inmortal;" "Dios;" "Pax;" Dulce Maria Loynaz, "La Oracion del Alba;" Clara Silva, "El Silencio de Dios;" from *Once Grandes Poetisas Americaohispanas*, edited by Carmen Conde, © 1967 by Ediciones Cultura Hispanica. Reprint permission requested of Ediciones Cultura Hispanica.

Ann Johnson, *Miryam of Nazareth: Women of Strength and Wisdom*, © 1984 by Ave Maria Press, Notre Dame, IN 46556. All rights reserved. Reprinted by permission of Ave Maria Press.

R. S. Loomis and R. Willard, "The Divine Paradox," from *Medieval English Verse and Prose in Modernized Versions*, © 1984 by Appleton-Century-Crofts, Inc. Reprinted by permission of Appleton-Century-Crofts, Inc.

Frederico Garcia Lorca, *Selected Poems*, © 1955 by New Directions Publishing Corporation. Reprinted by permission of New Directions Publishing Corporation.

Susanna March, "Amor," from *Antologia de la Nueva Poesia Espanola*, 3rd edition, edited by J. L. Cano, © 1972 by Camara del Libro (Spain). Reprint permission requested of Camara del Libro (Spain).

Gabriela Mistral, "Canciones de Solveig;" "La Casa;" "El Nino Solo;" "Himno al Arbol;" "La Mujer Esteril;" "Trigo Argentina;" from *Desolacion-Ternura-Tala-Lagar*, Introducion por Palma Guillen de Nicolau, "Sepan Cuantos . . . ," Num. 250, © 1986 by Editorial Porrua, S. A., Av. Republica Argentina. Reprint permission requested of Editorial Porrua, S. A., Av. Republica Argentina.

Gabriela Mistral, "Meciendo," from *Selected Poems of Gabriela Mistral*, translated by Doris Dana, © 1971 by Johns Hopkins Press. Reprint permission requested of Johns Hopkins Press.

Pablo Neruda, "Lamento Lento," from *Residencia en la Tierra*, 9th edition, ©
1958 by Editorial Losada, S. A. (Argentina). Reprinted by permission of the
Agencia Literaria Carmen Balcells, S. A. (Argentina).

Octavio Paz, "El Cantaro Roto," from *La Estacion Violenta*, fourth reprint, ©
1990 by Fondo de Cultura Economica (Mexico). Reprint permission requested
of Fondo de Cultura Economica (Mexico).

Carlos Rousano, "Cristo en la Tarde," from *Los Derechos del Hombre en la Poesia Hispanica Contemporanea*, edited by Manuel Mantero, © 1973 by Editorial Gredos, S. A. (Spain). Reprint permission requested of Editorial Gredos, S. A.
(Spain).

Alexander Solzhenitsyn, *One Day in the Life of Ivan Denisovich*, translated by
Ralph Parker, © 1963, renewed 1991, by Penguin USA and Victor Gollancz,
Ltd. Reprinted by permission of Dutton, an imprint of New American Library,
a division of Penguin Books USA, Inc.

A Tagore Reader, edited by Amiya Chakravarty, © 1961 by MacMillan Publishing Company. Reprinted by permission of MacMillan Publishing Company.

Mary Webb, *Precious Bane*, © 1980 by University of Notre Dame Press. Reprint
permission granted by University of Notre Dame Press.

Reference Works Consulted

The Anchor Bible, 44 volumes, edited by D. N. Freedman, © continuing by Ban-
tam Doubleday Publishing Group.

Bartlett's Familiar Quotations, 15th edition, edited by Emily Morison Beck, © 1980
by Little, Brown and Company.

The Dead Sea Scrolls in English, 3rd edition, translated by G. Vermès, © 1987
by Pelican Books.

Hermeneia: A Critical and Historical Commentary on the Bible, edited by F. M. Cross
and Helmut Koester, © continuing by Fortress Press.

The Loeb Classical Library, 479 volumes, © continuing by Harvard University
Press.

The New American Bible, © 1970 by Catholic Press.

The Oxford Dictionary of Quotations, 3rd edition, © 1990 by Oxford University
Press.

The Oxford Shakespeare, Complete Works, edited by Stanley Wells and Gary Tay-
lor, © 1991 by Clarendon Press.

The Old Testament Pseudepigrapha, 2 volumes, edited by James H. Charlesworth,
© 1983, 1985 by Doubleday.

The Quotable Lewis: An Encyclopedic Selection of Quotes from the Complete Published Works of C. S. Lewis, edited by Wayne Martindale and Jerry Root, © 1989 by Tyndale House Publishers.

A Rabbinic Anthology, edited by C. G. Montefiore and H. Loewe, © 1963 by Meridian Books, World Publishing Company.

The Soncino Talmud, E. T. 18 volumes, edited by I. Epstein, © commencing 1961 by Soncino Press.

Preface

God is to me
- Friend
  - Artist
    - Musician
      - Theologian
        - Democrat

God is to me *friend* because s/he is a companion in the adventure of life. I am bonded with the Immortal in a covenant relationship the essence of which is intimate love, freedom, nonintrusiveness and shared joy and pain. We have grown up together. We have passed through years of intense and demanding piety, in some sense the artless worship offered to a transcendent deity. I relinquished for her/him all I possessed. I entered the poorest religious community that I could find to serve the third world with the magic of medical science. God rejected my offer. S/he allured me into more arduous fields untrod by women. Like Abraham and Sarah s/he asked me to leave my native land but s/he gave me supporting friends at various points on the journey. I became the object of conflicting views: some scoffed, some encouraged. Yet in the bleakest moments s/he was there to succour, in the elation of success, s/he was there to rejoice with me. S/he allowed me to make my mistakes, laughed over them and found some redeeming features in them which would heal and nourish. S/he has been with me on occasions of acute physical pain and near death experiences and s/he has pointed to a life beyond, as mysterious as it is real.

And through all this time s/he kneaded, refined and fashioned a new image of herself/himself for me. It was as if s/he descended step by step from her/his transcendent throne and gave to me the reflection of the kaleidoscope of her/his immanence in all the crevices, holy and unholy, of this world. S/he taught me to find her/his sacramental presence in a creation, graced and graceless.

God reveals herself/himself to me in the multifarious ways of life. In this age of cacophony I hear her/him in silence; in this age of human manufacture I find her/him in the jocund wind in the trees, in the liberating ecstasy of my malamute as he prances in the woods, in tutelary care of my mare for her foal. Mounted on Equus I find her/him in the life surging through my veins from equine movement beneath me, like D. H. Lawrence's Brangwyns, I "hold life between my knees."

God exceeds the definition of creator laboriously debated in theological tomes, for s/he is supreme *artist*. With meticulous and infinite finesse s/he planned each atom of the universe. The author of Job understood this full well. Who, I ask, can equal God's creativity, her/his ingenuity, her/his colour schemes or the paradoxical nature of many of her/his creatures? We live surrounded by majestic mystery. We are blind and deaf. God is *musician*, conductor of the great orchestra of sound, human, animal and cosmic—if we have ears unphoned to hear! Who could compete with her/his avion choir? S/he has appointed us caretakers, stewards of this cosmos. We scale the heights of the moon and seek other planets. Yet, often, we are warmakers, not peacemakers. We perpetrate murder not only upon human beings but upon trees and plants and we poison the fruitful harvest of the sea.

God's mysterious presence pervades nature but s/he becomes starkly incarnate in the bewildering diversity of multicoloured human beings which s/he created. S/he is reflected in the mobile wrinkles of Mother Theresa; in the dismembered body of the leper; in the physical beauty, insouciance and hope of youth; in the quick body of the unborn.

Her/his presence here is no abstraction. S/he entered history and the human community in the person of Her/His Son, Jesus. He came as *theologian*, a graduate of the school of life and of Jewish wisdom, "middleclass," realist, perspicacious. He may have surrendered his wealth to identify with the poor and to set an example for the rich. He came to exegete (interpret) God (cf. John 1:18) in word and in deed. He was experienced in the unrivalled didactic power of his parables. He is seen as the itinerant exegete of Scripture on the road to Emmaus. But He was not only a theoretician. He accomplished his field research by identifying with the most degraded, abused and jested of humankind. He accepted the most obscene death—that of a slave. Thus he can empathize with the exploited poor, for his blood is shed in every victim of oppression. He knows the homelessness of the refugee and the clean teeth of the hungry. By his resurrection from the dead he taught us to have hope in despair, gain life through death, and "that there are more things in heaven and earth than are dreamt in thy philosophy . . ." (words of the immortal bard).

God is a *democrat*. As sovereign of sovereigns s/he neither dictates nor coerces. S/he is brutally honest. The members of her/his realm are free citizens whose conduct should be governed by responsibility to the community of humankind, respect for the human person and genuine feal love for their sovereign. Only those who have identified with her/him are true leaders of the people.

God is master/mistress of communication arts, chief of which is her/his Spirit. This Spirit co-opts human talents and human fallibility when s/he speaks through the pages of Scripture. S/he manages to be heard in spite of the peccability of Tradition. S/he comes as constant innovator, impatient of vegetating stasis, yet observer of the constant norm which preserves the *shalom* of Church and State. To imbibe her/him is to drink from the inexhaustible well of freedom and refreshment. S/he comes in the coolness of baptismal water to make all priests of God and of her/his Christ. S/he hovers over the jubilation and strife of marriage. S/he is host(ess) in the feast of reconciliation honouring the prodigal. S/he comes like peace-bearing balm through the anointing of the aged and the infirm. S/he presides in the resurrected presence of the Christ in the breaking of sacred bread.

This is God to me. What is God to you?

At a time when many of us meditate upon new models and images for God, I offer the above reflection. It is not scholarly but devotional. And it is in such a mood that I have composed the scriptural reflections on the daily Eucharistic readings in this commentary. I was delighted, some time ago, when Mr. Michael Glazier asked me to bring together some poetical and literary reflections on the lectionary. Although the Scriptures are our chief source of inspiration, it seems to me that the Holy Spirit enlightens us through many and diverse "theophanies" (appearance of the divine) and in our age we must recognize and accept these. Thus *Days of the Spirit* celebrates the fruits of the Spirit in all the humanities and unites these to the Sacred Text.

Mr. Glazier asked for about one page for each day. I have tried to adhere to this, especially as I hope that this book might help the busy professional person, the time-denied parent and, perhaps, even those not drawn to the Christian faith. Each day reflects on one reading or on one theme common to two or all three readings. When I have been unable to comment on one lesson in the reflection I have tried to include a thought from it in the intercessory prayers. The collects at the end are my own composition. This book is dedicated to my first and foremost American friend, Dr. Suzanne Kelly. We were the first two women on the teaching faculty at Notre Dame University and in our early years we shared an office. Suzanne's courageous, buoyant spirit was a tower of strength to me. She shared in that new breath of the Spirit which blew through the church by the inspiration of Pope John

XXIII of treasured memory. With wisdom, fortitude and humour she ploughed new ground in the church and the university. She celebrates life in a myriad ways. She is a superb mentor of many, not least of myself.

J. Massyngbaerde Ford
Easter, 1994

Introduction to Advent

Advent is a season of mystery which hovers between light and darkness and between the past, present and future. It carries a spirit of rejoicing blended with a spirit of penitence and holy fear. We look back to the Hebrew Scriptures, especially to the prophets of old, and try to comprehend God's meticulous plan of salvation, maturing over the ages and blossoming in all its glory in the coming of Christ. The understanding of this mystery requires spiritual sensitivity and insight rather than academic prowess. Yet in Advent we seek to look even beyond the birth and life of God's Anointed and our eyes search for the signs of the last days. We contemplate the destruction of evil and we hear the message of repentance and warning. We dream of an utopian world, a new, prolifically fertile earth and harmony between man, woman and beast. We are told that even the heavens will be renewed. We are alerted to the coming of the Righteous One to usher in this epoch. We take stock of our spiritual estate. We widen our concept of salvation to embrace all creation. We meet God as a tiny baby and an impartial, omniscient Judge.

As we stand face to face with this God in the daily Eucharistic readings at Mass or in our private devotional time, the Spirit leads us to deepen our understanding of the identity of Jesus. We find that he cannot be adequately described as a politico-charismatic Messiah. We weave together the various expectations of this Coming One found in the pages of Scripture. He is the prophet like Moses (Deut 18:15); he is Elijah *redivivus,* come alive again (Mal 4:5); he is the priestly Messiah from the tribe of Levi (nonbiblical Jewish tradition); he is the priest like Melchizadek (Gen 14, Epistle to the Hebrews); he is the Servant of the Lord (Isa 42; 49; 50; 52–53) and he is the Son of Humanity (Dan 7:13-14). All these expected figures find their realization in Jesus Christ.

Moreover, the incarnation, God becoming human, for which we yearn in Advent, tells us in blunt terms that humanity and godhood are not two opposite ends of a spectrum. God does not desire to work

1

without human cooperation. Our Advent meditations must bear fruit. So the question arises, How do we use our new insights? Can we assist in

bringing light into the darkness;

stripping ourselves for the fray of service without the hindrance of sin or ignorance;

broadening our concept of salvation;

imitating Christ as Servant, Teacher, Son of Humanity;

renewing our earth and our heavens, the visible and the invisible;

assessing our fears and hopes before our implacable judge and our Saviour, Friend of Sinners and Marginalized People, before God,

the All-Merciful,

All-Compassionate,

All-Forgiving One,

a Gift-giver Incomparable?

J. Massyngbaerde Ford
Eastertide, 1994

1 First Sunday of Advent
Cycle A

Isa 2:1-5; Rom 13:11-14; Matt 24:37-44

An old, old sight, and yet somehow so young; aye, and not changed a wink since I first saw it, a boy, from the sandhills of Nantucket! The same!—the same!—the same to Noah as to me. There's a soft shower to leeward. Such lovely leewardings! They must lead somewhere—to something else than common land, more palmy than the palms.　　　　　(H. Melville, *Moby Dick*)

¡Ah!, el círculo perpetuo de la vida y la muerte.
Pero la vida, ahora mismo,
se precipita loca en cada grano de polvo,
y en la barca del canto, Noé de nuevo
repite el alfabeto de los seres, los nombres
de las cosas.
　　—Es que vuelve, decidme, el gran Diluvio?
　　　　　(Issac Felipe Azofeifa, ''Poema de la Bomba H con
　　　　el Proverbio de Una Madre India,'' *Los Derechos*, 151)

The New Year of the Church opens with three scriptural readings which are juxtapositioned in startling contrast. Isaiah presents a proleptic and ideal vision of God's presence at the centre of the world and all nations, filled with hunger for God's Word, streaming up to God's temple. In the second reading Paul believes that it is the eve of the dawn of salvation, salvation rather like Thompson's *Hound of Heaven* approaching with insistent step. He tries to jolt the Roman Christians out of their insouciant revelry. Matthew portrays the sudden advent of the Son of Humanity into a world indifferent to the Gospel message even in the face of cosmic catastrophe. The Gospel refers to the mythical hero, Noah (Gen 6–9). Noah and his family became literary paradigms for all those who remain faithful despite an environment

3

of pernicious moral turpitude and godlessness. I have chosen a passage which shows human fortitude in the midst of most bitter trials. The occasion was a Jewish mother who witnessed the torture and martyrdom of her seven sons in the persecution of Antiochus Epiphanes 175 B.C.E. It is an incredible witness to devoted motherhood.

> Not the sirens' melodies nor the sweet sounds of the children's voices charm their mother when they speak to her from amid the tortures . . . true daughter of God-fearing Abraham . . . More noble than men in fortitude and stronger than heroes in endurance! Like the ark of Noah, carrying the universe in the world-wide cataclysm and stoutly enduring the waves, so did you, guardian of the Law, buffeted on every side in the flood of the passions and by the mighty gales of your sons' torments, so did you by your perseverance nobly weather the storms that assailed you for religion's sake.   (4 Macc 15:21, 28-31)

Mary and Joseph may have had sentiments similar to this mother when Jesus (according to Matthew) was born near the end of the reign of Herod. This period was, indeed, a veritable blood bath. Herod even murdered members of his own family. Matthew tells us that Jesus' family fled to Egypt on account of this political unrest and for the safety of the child.

Intercessions

> For those ensnared by life's frivolities;
> For those who, in diverse ways, reveal God to us.

Prayer

> Covenant God,
>   you hung your war bow upside down in the sky.
> You made a covenant with Noah, his wife and family
>   and all living creatures
> that the world should not again be destroyed by flood.
>   Grant us, too, to remember
> our covenant with humankind and our mother earth
>   so that we destroy our weapons of destruction
> and o'erarch the earth with the rainbow of gentleness. Amen.

2 First Sunday of Advent
Cycle B

Isa 63:16-17, 19; 64:2-7; 1 Cor 1:3-9; Mark 13:33-37

*Does something molded say to its molder, "Why did you make
me like this"? Does a potter not have the right to make from the
same lump of clay one vessel for a lofty purpose and another for
a humbler one?* (Rom 9:20-21)

*Dime, sequía, piedra pulida por el tiempo sin dientes, por el
   hambre sin dientes,
polvo molido por dientes que son siglos, por siglos que son hambres,
dime, cántaro roto caído en el polvo, dime,
¿la luz nace frotando hueso contra hueso, hombre contra hombre,
   hambre contra hambre,
hasta que surja al fin la chispa, el grito, la palabra,
hasta que brote al fin el agua y crezca al árbol de anchas hojas de
   turquesa?*

(Octavio Paz, "El Cántaro Roto," *La Estación Violenta*,
[Mexico: Fondo de Cuertara Económica, 1990] 53)

The prophet, Isaiah, compares humankind to vessels made by a potter, that is, God. The symbol is apt for the potter shapes the clay with
her/his hands, molds it, solidifies it by fire and adds the final refine-
ments. The same symbol is used by the author of one of the hymns
found at Qumran, the Jewish settlement near the Dead Sea in the Ju-
dean desert and in Greco-Roman literature in the ancient world. For
example, Seneca writing to console Marcia, compares human nature
to a fragile vessel:

*Your son is dead . . . Toward this, at different paces, moves all
this throng that now squabbles in the forum, that looks on at the
theatres, that prays in the temples . . . This, clearly, is the meaning of that famous utterance ascribed to the Phythian oracle: know
thyself.* What is man (sic)? *A vessel that the slightest shaking,
the slightest toss will break.* (Seneca, *Ad Marciam*)

Victor Furnish (1984:278) points out that an earthenware vessel, in
contrast to glass or metal, is useful only when intact. When broken
it cannot be melted down or repaired. Each vessel is unique, thus one
takes great care of earthenware. God as potter and humankind as the
earthenware utensils are portrayed graphically in the Hymn Scroll from

the Dead Sea Scrolls: God has prepared our fragile nature for heavenly, deathless realms.

> I thank Thee, O Lord,
>   for Thou hast redeemed my soul from the Pit,
> and from the hell of Abaddon
>   Thou hast raised me up to everlasting height.
>
> I walk on limitless level ground,
>   and I know that there is hope for him (her)
> whom Thou hast shaped from dust
>   for the everlasting Council.
> Thou hast cleansed a perverse spirit of great sin
>   that it may stand with the host of the Holy Ones,
> and that it may enter into community
>   with the congregation of the Sons of Heaven.
> Thou hast allotted to man (woman) an everlasting destiny
>   amidst the spirits of knowledge,
> that he may praise Thy Name in a common rejoicing
>   and recount Thy marvels before all Thy works.
>
> And yet I, a creature of clay,
>   what am I?
> Kneaded with water,
>   what is my worth and my might?
>   (1 Qumran Hymns 3, 5; trans. Vermès)

We may also compare Paul's words in 2 Corinthians 4:7-15 where he tells us that we carry our treasure in earthen vessels.

Intercessions

> For the gift of awareness, both with regard to matters divine and human;
>
> For forgiveness, that guilt be borne away by the breath of the Spirit.

Prayer

> God, whose hands are gentleness and strength,
>   your Son became an insignificant babe,
> whom many held in no esteem.
>   We beg you,
> never let us miss
>   treasures hidden in earthen vessels. Amen.

3 First Sunday of Advent
Cycle C

Isa 1:1-5; Rom 13:11-14; Matt 24:37-44

And on that day all the kings and the mighty and the exalted,
. . . will stand up. . . . And pain will come upon them as upon
a woman in labour for whom giving birth is difficult, when her
child enters the mouth of the womb, and she has difficulty in giv-
ing birth, and one half of them will look at the other, and they
will be terrified, and will cast down their faces, and pain will take
hold of them, when they see that Son of a Woman sitting on the
throne of his glory. (1 Enoch 62:3-5)

Niño Dios, que lloras naciendo:
perlas y flechas tus lágrimas son;
con las perlas redimes mis culpas,
con las flechas me hieres de amor.

Llora, llora, que el llanto,
partido en dos efectos diferentes,
hace que crezcan tanto
que perlas se admiren y flechas ardientes.

O inaccesible Grandeza de Dios!
Con las perlas redimes mis culpas,
con las flechas me hieres de amor.

(Sor Juana Inés de la Cruz, *Obras Completas*, 330)

Jesus speaks of unprecedented cosmic events—these are often described in terms of childbirth. We have a graphic example in the Dead Sea Scrolls.

Hymn Column 3.4.12, 18

. . . like a woman in travail
  with her first-born child,
  upon whose belly pangs have come
  and grievous pains,
filling with anguish her child-bearing crucible.

For the children have come to the throes of Death,
  and she labours in her pains who bears a man.
For amid the throes of Death
  she shall bring forth a man-child,

and amid the pains of Hell
  there shall spring from her child-bearing crucible,

a Marvelous Mighty Counsellor;
  and a man shall be delivered from out of the throes.

Through awesome travail the community writhes in the throes of childbirth to bring forth the Son of Justice who alone can bring security. There is no security unless it is based on justice.

Intercessions

For nations in the throes of giving birth to just leaders.

Prayer

God of Compassion,
  Come with your healing mercy
    to those bruised by human conflict,
      those confused by bereavement,
        those destitute by flood, fire or earthquake.
          Remember us
            when we are broken
              by trivialities. Amen.

176 Monday of the First Week of Advent

Isa 2:1-5 and Matt 8:5-11

Like choice silver is the just one's tongue. . . .
The just one's lips nourish many . . .
but the tongue of the wise is healing . . .
The tongue of the wise pours out knowledge. . . .
A soothing tongue is a tree of life. . . .
                              (Prov 10:20, 31; 12:18; 15:2, 4)

Si la voz se sintiera con los ojos
¡ay, cómo te vería!
Tu voz tiene una luz que me ilumina,
luz de oír.
Al hablar,
se encienden los espacios del sonido,

se le quiebra al silencio
la gran oscuridad que es. Tu palabra
tiene visos de albor, de aurora joven,
cada día, al venir a mí de nuevo.
(Pedro Salinas, *The Penguin Book of Spanish Verse*, 431)

In the first reading we hear of the nations streaming up to Jerusalem to hear the Word of God and in the second we see the faith of the Roman officer who believed in the power of the word of Jesus. Language is not just articulated sound; every spoken word carries a dynamism for good or ill, for blessing or curse. If this is true of ordinary speech how much more of the Word of God.

> *The Bible bears witness to a proclamation which has taken place and is the impulse to a proclamation which is to take place. And this event, which claims to be the Word of God, is not mere speech. But it sets something in motion, just as it itself was set in motion. It has to do with reality, which it changes.*
> (Robert W. Funk, *Language, Hermeneutics, and the Word of God: The Problem of Language in the New Testament* [New York: Harper and Row, 1966] 25)

Speech can be a curse, which is essentially verbal abuse with devastating effect or it can be a blessing, a vehicle of vitality which is constructive, creative, nourishing and unifying.
Compare the words of James:

> *Not many of you should become teachers . . . for you should realize that those of us who do so will be called to stricter account. . . . The tongue is a small member but it makes great pretensions. See how tiny the spark is that sets a huge forest ablaze. The tongue is such a flame. It exists among our members as a whole universe of malice. The tongue defiles the entire body. . . . We use it to curse people, though they are made in the image of God. Blessing and cursing come out of the same mouth.* (Jas 3:1-10)

We might also compare some nonbiblical Jewish literature:

> *Practice speaking the right word, which will greatly benefit all;*
> *Speech is to man a weapon sharper than iron.*
> *God allotted a weapon to every creature; the capacity to fly*
> *to birds, speed to horses, and strength to the lions;*

he clothed the bulls with their self-growing horns,
he gave stings to bees as their natural means of defense,
but speech to man (woman) as his (her) protection.

(Pseudo-Phocylides)

In Advent we seek to make our speech creative and curative. In doing so we confess our belief in dynamism of the Word, as did the centurion.

Intercessions

That weapons of destruction in this nuclear age might be beaten
into instruments of peace;

That we might exercise a faith like that of the centurion.

Prayer

O God,
your spoken Word brought creation out of chaos.
To humankind you have allotted
the awesome power of speech.
Grant us to use this treasure aright,
to temper it with wisdom;
to strengthen it with reason;
to sweeten it with gentleness.
May it be the balm that heals
the discordant cries
of a world out of tune with its Creator.
May human voices from all nations blend
into an orchestra of mutual harmony,
through Jesus Christ, the Word Incarnate. Amen.

177 Tuesday of the First Week of Advent

Isa 11:1-10 and Luke 10:21-24

The Centipede

With innumerable little footsteps
I go through life
but, Lord,
I can never
get to the end of myself!
It's a queer sensation
to be a multitude
that follows itself
in Indian file!
True,
it's the first step that counts
or, rather,
the first foot.
All that matters
is to be in step
with one's self.
I only ask,
Lord,
to jog along
one in spirit
without troublesome
reticences.

Amen.

(Carmen Bernos de Gasztold, *The Creatures' Choir*, trans.
Rumer Godden, New York: Viking Press, 1965, 23)

La espesa rueda de la tierra
su llanta húmeda de olvido
hace rodar, cortando el tiempo
en mitades inaccessibles.

Sus copas duras cubren tu alma
derramada en la tierra fría
con sus pobres chispas azules
volando en la voz de la lluvia.

(Pablo Neruda, "Lamento Lento"
Residencia en la Tierra, 25–26)

The first reading portrays an ideal picture of cosmic harmony. This is implemented by the intellectual gifts of the Spirit. These are certainly not confined to the academically wise. A well-known passage from Shakespeare's *Merchant of Venice* speaks about the harmony which is both in the universe and in human souls. This harmony should also be found not only within the individual but among communities, and the centipede quotation above speaks to both phenomena.

> . . . *How sweet the moonlight sleeps upon this bank!*
> *Here will we sit, and let the sounds of music*
> *Creep in our ears; soft stillness, and the night,*
> *Become the touches of sweet harmony.*
> *Sit Jessica. Look how the floor of heaven*
> *Is thick inlaid with patines of bright gold.*
> *There's not the smallest orb which thou behold'st*
> *But in his motion like an angel sings,*
> *Still quiring to the young-eyed cherubims:*
> *Such harmony is in immortal souls;*
> *But whilst this muddy vesture of decay*
> *Doth grossly close it in, we cannot hear it . . . .* (5.1.54–65)

> *The man that hath no music in himself,*
> *Nor is not moved with concord of sweet sounds,*
> *Is fit for treasons, stratagems, and spoils;*
> *The motions of his spirit are dull as night,*
> *And his affections dark as Erebus:*
> *Let no such man be trusted. Mark the music.* (5.1.83–88)

Intercessions

For harmony in our world;

For uncluttered lives;

For the unlettered.

Prayer

God, Great Conductor of the Orchestra of the Universe,
*   open our ears to the music of our world.*
Forgive us that we rape your innocent earth
*   and stifle the cries for justice.*
Quench our greedy thirst for gain
*   with the magnimity of your Spirit.*
Gentle the hands of our violence
*   and raise the poor of the world*
to be our tutors. Amen.

178 Wednesday of the First Week of Advent

Isa 25:6-10 and Matt 15:29-37

He was outcast from life's feast. (James Joyce, *Dubliners*)

*Strange to see how a good dinner and feasting reconciles every-
body.* (Samuel Pepys)

*Aquel pan, amasado en el dolor, crecido en la expectativa, cocido
con sudor y comido con alegría, es un símbolo fundamental de la
vida . . . Nadie como el (el papa) gozaba tanto del sabor de la ex-
istencia simple en la frugalidad generosa de estos alimentos primor-
diales de la humanidad.*
(Leonardo Boff, *Los Sacramentos de La Vida*, 8th ed. Coleccion
Alcance 1, Santander, Spain: Editorial Sal Terrae, 1989, 35)

The first reading speaks about the generosity of God's gifts in the
last days: it uses the symbols of feasting and drinking. Both the first
and second reading assure the reader that all will be invited, rich and
poor, Jew and Gentile, man, woman and child. No one will be an outcast from "Life's feast" as Joyce expresses it. The quotation from Pepys is well illustrated by the recent film *Babette's Feast*. Here a refugee
from Paris finds herself in a lonely village comprising a religious community, grown surly and contentious among themselves. She wins
a great sum of money and uses it all to prepare an exquisite meal. The
small, ardent but querulous religious community in this isolated village in Holland achieves internal harmony and love through this feasting. The film is a parable of the Eucharist which produces unity within
a disgruntled community.

Intercessions

For a feast for God's poor;

For a spirit of thanksgiving and wonder for God's gifts.

Prayer

God of Mirth and Joy,
we pray for those cast out of life's feast,
and for those blind to life's joys.
Implant in all humankind the joy of learning,
the thrill of discovery,
the humanity of the arts,

and a glimpse of that eternal feast
  where there will be a complete union
    among humankind
      and between God and humanity. Amen.

179 Thursday of the First Week of Advent

Isa 26:1-6 and Matt 7:21, 24-27

The honour'd gods
Keep Rome in safety, and the chair of justice
Supplied with worthy men! plant love among us!
Throng our large temples with the shows of peace,
And not our streets with war!

(Shakespeare, *Coriolanus*, 3.3.34–38)

Allí también viví, allí, ciudad graciosa, ciudad honda.
Allí donde los jóvenes resbalan sobre la piedra amable,
y donde las rutilantes paredes besan siempre
a quienes siempre cruzan, hervideros, en brillos.

(Vicente Aleixandre, "Ciudad del Paraíso,"
Penguin Book of Spanish Verse, 443)

The Lord said to Moses, "Tell the Israelites. When you go across the Jordan into the land of Canaan, select for yourselves cities to serve as cities of asylum, where a homicide who has killed someone unintentionally may take refuge. These cities shall serve you as place of asylum from the avenger of blood, so that a homicide shall not be put to death unless he is first tried before the community." (Num 35:9-12)

In Jewish history a city was distinguished from a village by having a defensive wall. The walls were massively built, often double in width and accommodating guard rooms and "court" rooms for hearing civil cases. So justice was administered at the gate. For example, the Israelite city of Jericho, perhaps some six thousand years old, has a huge wall with a round tower inside it. It was also important for a city to stand on a rock or high ground to make the defence easier. In times of war the people from the surrounding villages (the daughters of the city) would come to the city for protection. In addition Israel declared certain cities as asylums for those guilty of homocide.

In the Jewish Scriptures Jerusalem is the city *par excellence* and the Revelation of John portrays the new Jerusalem in the last days in two ways: firstly, as a walled city but built from precious stones (jewels) and secondly, as a bride coming down from heaven. Other early Christian writings speak of the chosen people as living stones (gems) of a living city. But we ourselves can also become ''cities of refuge'' for the needy as is shown in the following passage from an early Jewish Christian work.

> *And Asenath called the seven virgins. . . . And the man blessed them and said, ''May the Lord God the Most High bless you. And you shall be seven pillars of the City of Refuge and all the fellow inhabitants of the chosen of that city will rest upon you for ever (and) ever.''* (Joseph and Asenath 17:6)

Intercessions

> *For devastated cities;*
>
> *For the homeless;*
>
> *For the security which God's love can bring.*

Prayer

> *God, our Creator and Redeemer,*
>   *you did symbolize the rebuilding of Jerusalem*
> *as the work of an artist,*
>   *intricately wrought with precious and imperishable jewels.*
> *Grant to your chosen people,*
>   *through the inspiration of your Spirit,*
> *to rebuild with infinite care*
>   *the villages and cities*
> *devastated by natural catastrophe or by cruel war. Amen.*

180 Friday of the First Week of Advent

Isa 29:17-24 and Matt 9:27-31

> *O miserable minds of men! O blind hearts! In what darkness of life, in what great dangers ye spend this little span of years.*
> (Lucretius, *De Rerum Natura*)

Señores defensores de Ley y Orden:
¿Acaso el derecho de ustedes no es clasista?
   el Civil para proteger la propiedad privada
   el Penal para aplicarlo a las clases dominadas
La libertad de que hablan es la libertad del capital
  su ''mundo libre'' es la libre explotación
Su ley es de fusiles y su orden el de los gorilas
   de ustedes es la policía
   de ustedes son los jueces
No hay latifundistas ni banqueros en la cárcel.

        (E. Cardenal, Salmo 57, *Nueva Antología Poetica*,
        7th ed., Mexico: Siglo Veintiuno editores, 1988, 98)

The first lesson and the gospel today both speak of the blind. The Sacred Scriptures also use "blind" in a symbolic sense. In Shakespeare's *King Lear* we find a deep understanding of this. It is a scene in which the mad King Lear speaks with Gloucester who has been brutally blinded.

. . . A man may see how this world goes, with no eyes. Look with thine ears; see how yon' justice rails upon yon' simple thief. Hark, in thine ear; change places; and, handy-dandy, which is the justice, which is the thief? . . .

Through tatter'd clothes small vices do appear;
Robes and furr'd gowns hide all. Plate sin with gold,
And the strong lance of justice hurtless breaks;
Arm it with rags, a pigmy's straw doth pierce it.
None does offend, none, I say none; I'll able 'em:
Take that of me, my friend, who have the power
To seal the accuser's lips. Get thee glass eyes;

And, like the scurvy politician, seem
To see things thou does not. . . .

        (*King Lear*, 4.5.146–150, 160–168)

Intercessions

For those who pass unjust sentences;

For the tortured;

For an insight like the blind.

Prayer

> God of the Lowly,
> you have taught us
> that the "poor in the eyes of the world"
> are often rich in faith and heirs of the kingdom.
> Make us acutely aware of injustice in every form.
> Remove from our society and church every vestige of slavery
> and teach us wherein to find true sight. Amen.

181 Saturday of the First Week of Advent

Isa 30:19-21, 23-26; Matt 9:35–10:1, 5a, 6-8

In God's name, cheerly on, courageous friends,
To reap the harvest of perpetual peace . . .
(Shakespeare, Richard III, 5.2.14–15)

Segadores, ¡afuera, afuera!:
dejen llegar a la espigaderuela.

Si en las manos que bendigo
fuera yo espiga de trigo,
que me hiciera harina digo
y luego torta o bondigo,
porque luego me comiera.

Segadores, ¡afuera, afuera!:
dejen llegar a la espigaderuela.
(Francisco de Mediano, "Tirso de Molina,"
Penguin Book of Spanish Verse, 309)

Unlike our world which often takes no thought about wasting supplies, there was among people in the ancient world the concept of limited goods; that is, there was only limited resources to be distributed to all. Hence we find in much crisis literature the dream of a miraculous abundant fertility and supplies over and above daily needs. Thus apocalyptic writers particularly planted the seeds of hope of a renewed earth and prolific fertility in the life to come. This is one example of their dreams:

The earth also shall yield its fruit ten thousand-fold; and on each vine there shall be a thousand branches, and each branch shall produce a thousand clusters, and each cluster produce a thousand grapes, and each grape produce a cor of wine. And those who have been hungry will rejoice; and, also, they shall see marvels every day. For the winds shall go forth from me bearing the scent of aromatic fruits every morning, and, at the close of day, clouds distilling a health-giving dew. And at that time the storehouse of manna shall descend from on high again; and they shall eat of it in those years, because it is they who have come to the final consummation.

(Syriac Baruch 29)

A different view is expressed in Mary Webb's exquisite novel, *Precious Bane* (Indiana: South Bend Notre Dame University Press, 1980). This was awarded a French National Prize, "given annually for the best work of imagination in prose or verse descriptive of English life by an author who had not attained sufficient recognition" (10). Reflecting on sowing and reaping, the heroine, Prue Sarn says:

Gideon and me walking up and down the fields with the bags of seed slung over shoulder, or with a deep round lid to hold enough of seed for one crossing of the field there and back, and swinging out our arms with a great giving movement, as if we were feeding all the world, a thing I dearly loved to see. For reaping, though it is good to watch as be all the year's doings on a farm, is a grutching and a grabbing thing compared with sowing. You must lean out to it and sweep it in to you, and hold it to your bosom, jealous, and grasp it and take it. There is ever a greediness in reaping with the sickle, in my sight. There is not in scything, which is a large destroying movement without either love or anger in it, like the judgments of God. Nor is there in flailing, which is a thing full of anger, but without any will or wish to have or keep. But reaping is all greed, just as sowing is all giving. For there you go, up and down the wide fields, bearing that which you have saved with so much care, winnowing it from the chaff, and treasuring it for this hour. And though it is all you have, you care not, but take it in great handfuls and cast it abroad, with no thought of holding back any. On you go, straight forward, and the bigger your hand the better pleased you are, and you cast it away on this side and on that, till one not learned in country ways would say, here is a mad person (252).

Intercessions

For clarity of spiritual vision;

For the wound-binding of the oppressed;

For the unoppressed.

Prayer

God of Sowing and Reaping,
help us toward
"the harvest of perpetual peace,"
not by "bloody trial of sharp war,"
but by mutual reciprocity
and gallantry of heart. Amen.

4 Second Sunday of Advent
Cycle A

Isa 11:1-10; Rom 15:4-9; Matt 3:1-12

O villains, vipers, damn'd without redemption!
(Shakespeare, *Richard II*, 3.2)

Dear earth, I do salute thee with my hand,
Though rebels wound thee with their horses' hoofs:
As a long-parted mother with her child
Plays fondly with her tears and smiles, in meeting;
So, weeping-smiling, greet I thee, my earth . . .
Feed not my sovereign's foe, my gentle earth . . .
But let thy spiders, that suck up thy venom,
And heavy-gaited toads, lie in their way . . .
And when they from thy bosom pluck a flower,
Guard it, I pray thee, with a lurking adder,
Whose double tongue may with a mortal touch
Throw death upon thy sovereign's enemies . . . .
(Shakespeare, *Richard II*, 3.2.6–22)

La verdad religiosa
  y la verdad política
eran para el pueblo una misma verdad
Una economía con religión
  las tierras del Inca eran aradas por último
primero las del Sol (las del culto)
después las de viudas y huérfanos
después las del pueblo
  y las tierras del Inca aradas por último. . . .

(E. Cardenal, "Economía de Tahuantinsuyu,"
Nueva Antología, 150–51)

In the first reading Isaiah, the prophet, predicts the ideal age of peace when there will be complete harmony between humankind and the animal kingdom. The theme of harmony is taken up also by Paul in the second reading. But in the gospel reading we hear John the Baptist's harsh words of reproach to the Jewish leaders. He calls them "a brood of vipers." The graphic image portrayed is one of snakes fleeing from a ravaging harvest or forest fire. The viper is a symbol of the venom of deceitful, uncharitable and destructive speech and conduct. But John is not speaking about a viperous individual but of a community or, at least, a group, especially a group with power. Similarly the Dead Sea Scroll community thought of a malicious people as giving birth to a venomous snake.

Hymn Column 3:12, 18

And She who is big with the Asp is prey to terrible anguish . . .
and the doors of the Pit close upon her who is big with Perversity,
and everlasting bars upon all the spirits of the Asp.

(trans. Dupont-Somer)

There are not a few governments today who behave like vipers vis-à-vis the poorer people.

Intercessions

For those in authority that they may never degrade themselves with falsehood;

For reverence for our mother earth.

Prayer

> *God of Truth,*
> *help us to be acutely aware of*
> *the lethal nature of deceit,*
> *through Jesus Christ who is the Way, the Truth*
> *and the Life. Amen.*

5 Second Sunday of Advent
Cycle B

Isa 40:1-5, 9-11; 2 Pet 3:8-14; Mark 1:1-8

What plea so tainted and corrupt,
But, being seasoned with a gracious voice,
Obscures the show of evil. (Shakespeare, *Merchant*, 3)

Earth is but the frozen echo of the silent voice of God.
(S. M. Hageman, *Silence*)

Desde el umbral de un sueño me llamaron . . .
Era la buena voz, la voz querida.
—Dime: ¿vendrás conmigo a ver el alma? . . .
Llegó a mi corazón una caricia.

—Contigo siempre . . . Y avancé en mi sueño
por una larga, escueta galería,
sintiendo el roce de la vesta pura
y el palpitar suave de la mano amiga.
(Antonio Machado, "Galerías,"
Penguin Book of Spanish, 415)

The reading from the Hebrew Scriptures describes a voice which re-assures, comforts, forgives and invites us to new opportunities for hope. It encourages us to look forward to forgiveness, reconciliation and joy. In the New Testament reading we hear of the people flocking to John in response to his message from God. We are accustomed to see John as a fierce figure with an imperious and even condemnatory voice. But a voice which offers forgiveness and announces the advent of a powerful and concerned leader, who cares for his people as a shepherd cares for his sheep, is not necessarily a harsh one. Might the clothing of the Baptist be ascetic in appearance but might not his voice be rich with mercy? Francis Thompson in her poem "Hound of Heaven" describes the soul who flees from God's invitation but is obliged to cede to his persistence and the majesty of his voice.

> *I fled Him, down the nights and down the days;*
> *I fled Him, down the arches of the years;*
> *I fled Him, down the labyrinthine ways*
> *Of my own mind; and in the mist of tears*
> *I hid from Him, and under running laughter . . . .*
> *But with unhurrying chase,*
> *And unperturbed pace,*
> *Deliberate speed, majestic instancy,*
> *They beat—and a Voice beat*
> *More instant than the Feet—*
> *All things betray thee, who betrayest Me.*
>
> (Francis Thompson, *Hound of Heaven*)

The voice that captivates us is the voice of love, God's love for his Chosen people. Many poets speak of the power of the voice, for example:

> *All love is sweet,*
> *Given or returned. Common as light is love,*
> *And its familiar voice wearies not ever. . . .*
>
> (Shelley, *Prometheus Unbound*)
>
> *The Devil hath not, in all his quiver's choice,*
> *An arrow for the heart like a sweet voice.*   (Byron, *Don Juan*)

Intercessions

> *For the gift of listening;*
>
> *For those who echo God's voice.*

Prayer

> *God, who spoke and the world emerged from chaos,*
>   *teach us the art of graceful speech*
> *that we may draw, even from the hardest heart,*
>   *an expression of love. Amen.*

6 Second Sunday of Advent
Cycle C

Bar 5:1-9; Phil 1:4-6, 8-11; Luke 3:1-6

And homeless near a thousand homes I stood,
And near a thousand tables pined and wanted food.
(Wordsworth, Guilt and Sorrow)

That is my home of love: if I have rang'd,
Like him that travels, I return again.
(Shakespeare, Sonnet 109, 1. 5)

La mesa, hijo, está tendida,
en blancura quieta de nata,

. . .

Ésta es la sal, éste el aceite
y al centro el Pan que casi habla.
(Gabriela Mistral, "La Casa," Desolación,
Ternura—Tala—Lagar, 89)

Today's reading speaks of homecoming, the triumphant and exultant return of the Jewish exiles from Babylonia. Uprooted from their land, their sacred temple destroyed and their king dying a brutal death, the Jewish people were deported to Babylonia in the sixth century B.C.E. Psalm 137 is an eloquent witness to their longing for home:

By the streams of Babylon
  we sat and wept
when we remembered Zion . . .
  Though there our captors asked of us
  the lyrics of our songs . . .
  How could we sing a song of the Lord
in a foreign land?

It is against this background that we should hear the first reading, the people's longing for their mother-city, Jerusalem.

Thucydides, a Greek historian, speaks thus of his native city, Athens.

Fix your eyes on the greatness of Athens as you have it before you day by day, fall in love with her, and when you feel her great, remember that her greatness was won by men (sic) with courage, with knowledge of their duty, and with a sense of honour in ac-

tion . . . For the whole earth is the sepulcher of famous men; and
their story is not graven only on stone over their native earth, but
lives on far away, without visible symbol, woven into the stuff of
other men's lives. For you now it remains to rival what they have
done and, knowing the secret of happiness to be freedom and the
secret of freedom a brave heart. . . .

(Thucydides, *History of the Peloponnesian War,*
"Funeral Oration of Pericles")

The Jews might have felt in a similar way about Jerusalem. What are
our feelings about our cities and homes?

Intercessions

For a joyful commitment to our families and nation;
For the grace of hospitality.

Prayer

God of Liberation, who led the great Exodus from Egypt,
raise up for our world
those men and women
who may guide all nations
to freedom and peace. Amen.

182   Monday of the Second Week of Advent

Isa 35:1-10; Luke 5:17-26

Little soul, wandering, gentle guest and companion of the
body. . . .   (Publius Aelius Hadrianus, *Ad Animam Suam*)

Escucho
el silencio de Dios,
el gran vacío
de su intención secreta.

(Clara Silva, "El Silencio de Dios," *Once Grandes*
Poetas Americohispanas, Madrid: Cultura Hispana, 379)

The first reading uses the symbol of the cure of a physical handicap—
blindness, deafness, and lameness—to illustrate spiritual healing. In

the gospel reading, we find Christ both healing physical paralysis and the sickness of sin. Jesus' physical healings were signs of that greater healing that can take place both here and now and in the world to come, a healing of the inner person. I quote two passages to illustrate this theme.

> *Beloved Pan, and all ye other gods who haunt this place, give me beauty in the inward soul; and may the outward and inward man be at one. May I reckon the wise to be wealthy, and may I have such a quantity of gold as none but the temperate can carry.*
> > (Plato, *Phaedrus*)

> *Beauty is momentary in the mind—*
> *The fitful tracing of a portal;*
> *But in the flesh it is immortal.*
> *The body dies; the body's beauty lives.*
> > (Wallace Stevens, *Peter Quince at the Clavier*)

Intercessions

> *For fertility in waterless lands;*
> *For the paralyzed in mind and body;*

Prayer

> *God our Creator,*
> > *teach your people*
> > > *not to limp and grope about in your world of beauty.*
> *Grant us agility of mind*
> > *and grace of body—*
> *to respond to your own artistry. Amen.*

183 Tuesday of the Second Week of Advent

Isa 40:1-11; Matt 18:12-14

> *So flies the reckless shepherd from the wolf;*
> *So first the harmless sheep doth yield his fleece,*
> *And next his throat unto the butcher's knife.*
> > (Shakespeare, *Henry VI*, 5.6.7–9)

¡Oh llama de amor viva
que tiernamente hieres
de mi alma en el más profundo centro,
pues ya no eres esquiva,
acaba ya, si quieres;
rompe la tela de este dulce encuentro!

> (San Juan de la Cruz, "Canción de la llama
> de amor viva," *Penguin Book of Spanish Verse,* 221)

Many contemporary Christians do not find the image of the shepherd attractive. For them the sheep are "brainless" and the shepherd is portrayed in a long, white garment holding a cuddly, white, woolly lamb. This is a false image. Shepherds were energetic, agile and courageous persons who defended their flocks against wild animals and robbers, often at the risk of their own lives. Further, in the Ancient Near East the word "shepherd" was a synonym for "ruler" and was an honourable title. In the ancient world, too, the god Tammuz (or Thammus) was the shepherd of the cosmic flocks, the stars. The shepherd was also the one who accompanied the souls to the Land of the Dead. He possessed supreme power. In this light we might read Hebrews 13:20-21

> *May the God of peace who brought up from the dead the Great Shepherd of the sheep by the blood of the eternal covenant, Jesus our Lord, furnish you with all that is good. . . .*
>
> (Heb 13:20-21, cf. 1 Pet 2:25; "the Shepherd,
> the guardian of your souls.")

Intercessions

For the life-giving breath of God;

For the return of those who have "disappeared" (desaparecidos) under military regimes.

Prayer

God, Faithful Shepherd of Israel,
teach us to be cherishing custodians
of those who are confused, chilled and pained
in the rough pastures of this world. Amen.

184 Wednesday of the Second Week of Advent

Isa 40:25-31; Matt 11:28-30

I shall with aged patience bear your yoke. . . .
(Shakespeare, *Pericles*, 2.4)

. . . (Yoke-fellow to his honour-owing wounds) . . .
(Shakespeare, *Henry V*, 4.6)

Carne de yugo, ha nacido
más humillado que bello,
con el cuello perseguido
por el yugo para el cuello.

Nace, como la herramienta,
a los golpes destinado,
de una tierra descontenta
y un insatisfecho arado.

Entre estiércol puro y vivo
de vacas, trae a la vida
un alma color de olivo
vieja ya y encallecida.
(Miguel Hernández, "El Niño Yuntero,"
Recent Poetry of Spain, 8)

A yoke was an iron or wooden frame worn by draft animals to pull heavy loads (cf. Jer 27:2). Yokes were also worn by people in order to carry heavy loads and distribute the weight more evenly. The yoke was a symbol of hardship and service or slavery but it could also be a metaphor for discipline and union. Because of its association with oxen it also symbolized sacrifice. The Jewish people spoke about the yoke of the Torah (Law) which they willingly received from God. There is a Russian proverb which says:
Wherever there is a neck there is a yoke.
This is true. But the yoke which Jesus placed upon our necks was "easy" and makes burdens lighter, distributing the weight. We should be in tune with the Jewish admonition which reads as follows: "Every yoke, afflictive and burdensome, which comes upon you, loose it for the Lord's sake, and you will receive a reward on the day of judgment."
(2 Enoch Appendix 2)

Intercessions

That the army of stars may lead us to wider visions;

That we might give strength to the faint.

Prayer

Jesus, your yoke is easy and your burden light,
look with compassion on those
yoked in discordant marriage,
yoked in cheerless labour,
yoked with monotonous years
and yoked to selfish gain.
Forgive us for enslaving others
and grant us true freedom in mind and body. Amen.

185   Thursday of the Second Week of Advent

Isa 41:13-20; Matt 11:11-15

He that plants trees loves others beside himself.
(Thomas Fuller: *Gnomologia*)

The finer the tree the more pliant the twig.   (Dutch Proverb)

A brotherhood of venerable trees . . . .
(Wordsworth, *Sonnet Composed at Castle*)

Arbol hermano, que clavado
por garfios pardos en el suelo,
la clara frente has elevado
en una intensa sed de cielo.
(Gabriela Mistral, "Himno al Arbol," *Desolación*, 97)

The prophet Isaiah, while the chosen people were in exile in Babylon, dreams of luxurious trees growing in the desert. He mentions *the acacia*, a hard but light-wooded tree that does not absorb moisture and therefore keeps its form and volume. (It was used for making the ark of the covenant.) He speaks of *the cedar*, a hardy, long-living, beautiful tree, known as the "tree of the Lord" (Ps 80:11; 1 Kgs 5:13; 2 Kgs 14:9; Ezek 31:3-7). He names *the myrtle*, a fragrant and glossy-leaved tree which bears blackberries. (The myrtle is an evergreen that the

rabbis compared to Esther, whose Hebrew name is "Hadassah"—
myrtle. Its branches were often used for bridal crowns.) Isaiah refers
to *the olive*, a tree which is said to produce fruit even when it is still
a thousand years old—cf. Judges 9:8-9; Jeremiah 11:16. (Olive shoots
protect the trunk from which they grow, and if this is cut down they
continue to grow. The tree itself is exquisitely grained, and its sprig
is a symbol of peace—Gen 8:11.) The prophet also speaks of *the pine*,
which is perhaps one of the most important trees, for it gives plenty
of shade—Sirach 50:10. (The pine tree grows near rivers and it is one
of the most beautiful of Israel's trees.)

The prophet Isaiah speaks as if all these trees would grow in the desert. But he is using an age-old symbol: the tree is a mature, spiritual
person who endures with great fortitude and towering strength. In
this vein Walt Whitman says:

> *How strong, vital, enduring! how dumbly eloquent! What sug-
> gestions of imperturbability and being, as against the human trait
> of mere seeming. Then the qualities, almost emotional, palpably
> artistic, heroic, of a tree; so innocent and harmless, yet so savage.*
> (Walt Whitman, *Specimen Days*)

Intercessions

> For forgiveness for God's church because she often tried to spread
>   the gospel by violence;
>
> For the unborn who have died by violence.

Prayer

> O God, venerable in your age old love,
>   let us be like trees,
>   reaching up, tall and straight, to your love
>   and bending like a willow to your gracious pleasure. Amen.

186 Friday of the Second Week of Advent

Isa 48:17-19; Matt 11:16-19

> *Then Heaven tries the earth if it be in tune,*
> *And over it softly her warm ear lays.*
> (Lowell, *Vision of Sir Launfal*)

La tierra es dulce cual humano labio,
como era dulce cuando te tenía,
y toda está ceñida de caminos . . .
Eterno amor, te espero todavía.

Miro correr las aguas de los años,
miro pasar las aguas del Destino.
Antiguo amor, te espero todavía:
la tierra está ceñida de caminos. . . .
(Gabriela Mistral, "Canciones de Solvieg," *Desolación,* 49)

Both readings today speak of listening and appropriate response. L. M. Alcott describes people who tune "to poetry Life's prose." In the short gospel reading, Jesus deplores people who never empathise with others. Like the insane Ophelia in *Hamlet* they are "like sweet bells jangled, out of tune and harsh" (Shakespeare, 3.1.16). They never tune themselves to the rhythm of another's life. Others adapt themselves to the needs and opportunities of the world around them and do, in the words of L. M. Alcott, tune "to poetry Life's prose." They realize that "no sound is dissonant which tells of life." (Coleridge, *Lime Tree Bower My Prison*)

Intercessions

For discernment in listening to the voice of God;

For a readiness to admit our mistakes.

Prayer

Creator of Cosmic Harmony,
  give to us a listening ear.
May we discern the rhythm of our world,
  the frail cries for justice;
the raw proclamation of ambition,
  the creaking sighs of bondage,
the arrogant jests of the surfeited.
  Lead us to that true melody,
    rich with liberation,
      prodigal with love,
        serene with justice
and pregnant with the seeds of peace. Amen.

187 Saturday of the Second Week of Advent

Sir 48:1-4, 9-11; Matt 17:10-13

R. Nathan met Elijah and asked him what God did in that hour.
Elijah replied, "He laughed and said, 'My children have conquered
me.' "   (Baba Mesia 59b)

El indio sube al templo tambaleándose,
ebrio de sus sollozos como de un alcohol fuerte.
Se para frente a Dios a exprimir su miseria
y grita con un grito de animal acosado
y golpea entre sus puños su cabeza. . . .

Repose largamente
tu inocencia de manos que no crucificaron,
Repose tu confianza
reclinada en el brazo del Amor
como un pequeño pueblo en una cordillera.
(Rosario Castellanos, "La Oración del Indio." *Poesia,* 67–68)

Elijah was a prophet of great renown among the chosen people and they expected him to return at the end of time, as is shown in the first reading. In history and tradition he is seen as the zealous opponent of the pagan religions promoted by Queen Jezebel (1 Kgs 19: 10,14). This is exemplified particularly in his great contest with the prophets of Baal (1 Kgs 18). There was a tradition that Elijah did not die but was carried to heaven in a chariot drawn by fiery horses (2 Kgs 2:1-11). His mantle fell on Elisha, his disciple so that he might carry on the work of Elijah. The prophet "wore the distinctive dress" a garment of haircloth, "with a girdle of leather about his loins" (2 Kgs 1:8) so that in external appearance John the Baptist resembles him.

It was in the messianic age that Elijah was expected to return (see Mal 3:23 and our first reading). He would solve legal problems and usher in a time of peace (*Eduyyot* 8:7). He would also announce the coming redemption and be an advocate for social justice. He is expected to punish the miserly and benefit the poor. At the Feast of Passover many Jews have a cup of wine ready and the door open for Elijah. When he arrives he will be placed in the centre of the table and will announce the coming Messiah.

R. Joshua b. Levi met Elijah . . . He said . . . "And what is
his (the Messiah's) mark? [How shall I recognise him?] He sits
among the wretched who are laden with sicknesses [sores and

wounds are meant, and it is implied that he, too, has sores and wounds]; all the others uncover all their wounds, and then bind them all up again, but he uncovers and binds up each one separately, for he thinks, 'Lest I should be summoned and be detained.'"

(Sanhedrin 98a)

Intercessions

That, like the Baptist, we may decrease so that Christ will increase;

That pioneers may accept their destiny to be rejected.

Prayer

God of the Prophets,
  help us to be open to the message of your friends,
and to accept it whether or not
  it reaches up to our expectations. Amen.

7 Third Sunday of Advent
Cycle A

Isa 35:1-6, 10; Jas 5:7-10; Matt 11:2-11

Silence is the perfectest herald of joy. . . .

(Shakespeare, *Much Ado*, 2.1)

"¡Libertad! ¡Libertad!," sonó en los cielos
mas no en el seno oscuro de la Tierra,
cayéronsele al siervo las esposas,
  rotas no, sino sueltas.

  . . .

¡Baja del cielo, Libertad sublime,
y humillándote al mundo hazte terrena,
rompe los grillos del derecho infame,
  y ensánchanos la Tierra!
(Miguel de Unamuno, "A la Libertad," *Los Derechos*, 249–50)

In the reading from Isaiah the herald announces freedom and comfort for the chosen people in their Babylonian captivity. In the gospel reading, John the Baptist is seen as the herald of the kingdom of God.

We know that from Homeric days the herald was a significant person. He had both political and religious importance. He occupied a place in the monarch's court as a personal friend and servant of the king. He was sent on diplomatic missions. He proclaimed the sovereign's messages, kept order in public meetings, and arranged ceremonies. He was under the protection of the god Hermes (among the Romans Mercury), who travelled in a broad brimmed hat, with durable sandals and a herald's staff as a sign of authority. Hermes was also thought to be the god of merchants or others who had to travel by road (there was always danger of bandits).

A herald was required to have a strongly resonant voice. Indeed, at the festival games there were often contests between heralds. He was also obliged to proclaim his message clearly and without fictitious embellishment. Sometimes he was required to plead the cause of the one who sent him. He often possessed the gifts of oratory and music and was regarded by all as a person of wisdom and sagacity. The herald was sacrosanct; it was sacrilegious to harm him. So Jesus' designation of the Baptist as a herald would be meaningful to the people.

But over and above the duties on a human level the herald was often seen as a messenger of the gods and goddesses. It was incumbent on him to bear witness to the revelation which the gods gave him. The Jewish rabbis used a word for herald which may have been derived from a Persian word for "cock." The herald, like the cock, calls people to wakefulness and activity. The early Christians were seen as eager heralds of the gospel of Jesus Christ. The immortal bard speaks eloquently about the brevity and punctuality required of a "herald."

> . . . I have learn'd that fearful commenting
> Is leaden servitor to dull delay;
> Delay leads impotent and snail-paced beggary:
> Then fiery expedition be my wing,
> Jove's Mercury, and herald for a king!
>> (Shakespeare, *Richard III*, 4.3.51–55)

Intercessions

That we may count it a privilege to care for the earth;

That the handicapped may have many friends.

Prayer

God of Good Tidings,
   grant that we may be authentic heralds of the gospel.

Let our words be brief but perspicacious;
  our bearing genteel,
    our humour contagious.

  Make our lives the most eloquent witness
  to the truth we proclaim. Amen.

8 Third Sunday of Advent
Cycle B

Isa 61:1-2, 10-11; 1 Thess 5:16-24; John 1:6-8, 19-28

I must have liberty
Withal, as large a charter as the wind,
To blow on whom I please.   (Shakespeare, *Henry V*, 4)

Rey de un trigal, de un río, de una viña:
así habrá de soñarse. Y libre. Dueño
de si, hoguera perpetua en que arda el leño
de la verdad. Y que el amor lo ciña.
                    (José Hierro, ''Niño,'' *Los Derechos*, 254)

The first reading speaks about the coming of the Jubilee year, inaugurated by the blowing of a trumpet. Leviticus 25:8-22 describes the original intent of this year of good favour. The land was to be distributed equally according to the number of members of each tribe. But, as is to be expected, it often came into the hands of the rich. So the Jubilee year was to be implemented every fiftieth year. In the Jubilee year, land was to be restored to its original owner(s); debts were to be remitted; slaves (Hebrew) were to be freed and, perhaps prisoners released. It was, therefore, a year of good favour for the poor. The main purpose of the Jubilee year was the redistribution of wealth so that there was no accumulation of riches and power into the hands of the few.

However, it is not known how often the Jubilee was really implemented. Gradually, it lost its socially orientated character and, even when the Christian church adopted it, she never returned to its true meaning but made it a year of pilgrimage. This was often financially rewarding for Rome. Advent invites us to reconsider all aspects of slavery and liberation and also a just distribution of land and wealth and release from one's own bondage. This is the true spirit of the Jubilee:

"No man is wholly free. He is a slave to wealth, or to fortune, or the laws, or the people restrain him from acting according to his will alone" (Euripides, *Hecuba*).

Prayer

> God, we confess yours is the world
>   and all the lands of the nations.
> We live as your tenants upon the earth,
>   help us so to fulfill our stewardship
> that we shall not be ashamed
>   when Christ comes in glory. Amen.

9 Third Sunday of Advent
Cycle C

Zeph 3:14-18; Phil 4:4-7; Luke 3:10-18

No fear can stand up to hunger, no patience can wear it out, disgust simply does not exist where hunger is; and as to superstition, beliefs, and what you may call principles, they are less than chaff in a breeze. (Joseph Conrad, *Heart of Darkness*)

The corn was orient and immortal wheat, which never should be reaped, nor was ever sown. I thought it had stood from everlasting to everlasting. (Thomas Traherne, *Centuries of Meditations*)

El pan está sobre el campo,
como grandes ropas, hijo,
azorado de abundancia,
de dichoso, sin sentido. . . .
(Gabriela Mistral, "Trigo Argentino," *Desolación*, 87)

The second reading uses a Jewish image of the Coming One winnowing the chaff from the wheat. Harvesting was manual labour, usually expensive in time and energy. After the crop was cut the kernels of the wheat had to be separated from the straw. The stalks were laid out on the threshing floor which was a flat surface of hard earth or rock. The farmer might beat them with a stick or use animals to trample over them or he might use a threshing tool made of wooden frame with metal or sharp stones. First, the farmer used a fanlike tool or a fork or shovel and then sifted the wheat to remove more of the waste from the kernels. He threw the stalks of the grain into the air so that the kernels would be separated from the chaff which the wind carried away. This process was usually performed on the threshing floor in the late afternoon or evening when there would be a wind (cf. Ruth 3:2). The grain fell near the worker, the straw was carried a little further away and the chaff flew off in the wind. Chaff was useless for anything but making fire (Genesis Rabbah 83:3). The granary comprised an entire building or silos or jars.

Thus the reading presents us with a bold metaphor for separating the good from the wicked (cf. Jer 15:7; 51:2). In the Bible chaff is a symbol of worthless people (Job 21:18; Ps 1:4; Isa 17:13; Hos 13:3; Zeph 2:2). After winnowing, the farmer stands guard until the wheat is taken to granary.

Thus today's reading does not speak about a quick judgment but a laborious, slow and meticulous one separating the good from the recalcitrant. John sees the Anointed One doing just this.

Intercessions

> That we may have patience to weigh all decisions;
> That God may be able to rejoice over us.

Prayer

> God of Harvest and Homecoming,
>   you will to gather all into your heavenly granary.
> Through the grace of your Spirit,
>   enable us to sift away all vanities
> so that we may discern that eternal wheat
>   which finds root only in the soil of integrity. Amen.

188 Monday of the Third Week of Advent*

Num 24:2-7; 15-17; Matt 21:23-27

The heavenly rhetoric of thine eye.
(Shakespeare, *Loves Labour Lost* 4.3.60)

Yo amo mis ojos y tus ojos y los ojos
Los ojos con su propia combustión
Los ojos que bailan al son de una música interna
Y se abren como puertas sobre el crimen
Y salen de su órbita y se van como cometas sangrientos al azar
Los ojos que se clavan y dejan heridas lentas a cicatrizar
Entonces no se pegan los ojos como cartas
Y son cascadas de amor inagotables
Y se cambian día y noche.
(Vicente Huidobro, "Canto IV," *Temblor de Cielo*, 100)

The first reading is remarkable. It shows an opponent of the chosen people giving a prophecy of encouragement and truth. Balaam was a folk hero who appears in both biblical and nonbiblical sources. Ancient people were fascinated by him as they were by Noah, Daniel and Job. He was accredited with the gifts of divination and prophecy. But traditions about him differ. The fable in Numbers 22:21-35 does not present him in a good light. He possesses less insight than his donkey and in Numbers 31:8,16 he causes Israel to sin at Baal-peor.

However, in our passage, Numbers 24:2-7, 15-17, he appears more favorable. Balak asks him to curse the Israelite army but he responds that he can only say what the Lord tells him and he pronounces a blessing instead. He also intimates the coming of the Anointed One.

We must listen attentively for God's Word and discern truth from falsehood and proclaim God's exact message, even if it is spoken by an opponent.

In the gray beginning of years, in the twilight of things that began, The word of the earth in the ears of the world, was it God? was it man?
(Swinburne, *Hymn of Man*)

*If today or any day in the Third Week of Advent falls on the 17 or 18 of December, go to no. 194 or 195, pp. 51 or 53.

Intercessions

*That oppressed nations may have kindled within them the flame
of hope;*

*That we may have the courage to proclaim our faith even in the
face of danger or unpopularity.*

Prayer

*All-seeing God,
  grant us the grace
    to hear and see your message
      when it comes through foe or misadventure. Amen.*

189   Tuesday of the Third Week of Advent

Zeph 3:1-2; 9-13; Matt 21:28-32

*Of insolence is bred
The tyrant; insolence full blown,
With empty riches surfeited,
Scales the precipitous bright and grasps the throne.
Then topples o'er and lies in ruin prove;
No foothold on that dizzy steep.
But o may Heaven the true patriot keep
Who burns with emulous zeal to serve the state.
God is my help and hope, on him I wait.*

*Más allá estan los campos y el camino de acacias
y la quinta suntuosa de aquel pobre señor
Millonario y obeso, que con todos sus oros
No podría comprarnos ni un gramo del tesoro
Inefable y supremo que nos ha dado Dios:
Ser flexibles, ser jóvenes, estar llenos de amor.*
(Juana de Ibarbourou, ''Millonarios,'' Los Derechos, 437)

The first reading denounces Israel's enemy, Babylon, who destroyed
Jerusalem and the temple and sent all the leading persons of Judah
into exile. The prophet, Zephaniah, foretells the fall of the tyrannical
city, and the gospel lesson shows that those who have precedence or
are considered socially more acceptable may find their places taken by

the "outcasts of Life's feast." Life is never without its tyrants in one form or another. When God or nature has sifted the nations the arrogant are blown away like chaff. We could quote a number of examples of the demise of successful men or women. One most potent example is Wolsey, portrayed by Shakespeare in *Henry VIII* 3.2:

> *Cromwell, I charge thee, fling away ambition;*
> *By that sin fell the angels; how can man then,*
> *The image of his Maker, hope to win by it?*
> *Love thyself last: cherish those hearts that hate thee;*
> *Corruption wins not more than honesty.*
> *Still in thy right hand carry gentle peace,*
> *To silence envious tongues. Be just, and fear not:*
> *Let all the ends thou aim'st be thy country's,*
> *Thy God's, and truth's; then if thou fall'st, O Cromwell,*
> *Thou fall'st a blessed martyr . . .*
> *Had I but served my God with half the zeal*
> *I had served my king, he would not in mine age*
> *Have left me naked to mine enemies . . .*
> *Farewell*
> *The hopes of court! my hopes in heaven do dwell.*

Intercessions

> *For the marginal people that they may enter God's kingdom with joy;*
> *For prostitutes that they may hear God's call.*

Prayer

> *Jesus, our Brother and our God,*
>   *who through the base cross was brought to glory,*
> *temper our boastful ambition. Amen.*

190   Wednesday of the Third Week of Advent

Isa 45:6-8, 18, 21-25; Luke 7:18-23

This even-handed justice. . . . (Shakespeare, *Macbeth*, 1.7.10)

Librame de sus Consejos de Guerra,
de la rabia de sus jueces y sus guardias.

Tú eres quien juzga a las grandes potencias.
Tú eres el Juez que juzga a los Ministros
de Justicia
Y a las Cortes Supremas de Justicia.

(Ernesto Cardenal, "Salmo 7," *Los Derechos,* 260)

The first reading speaks of the supreme, impeachable power of God. Especially moving are the lines:

Let justice descend, O heavens, like dew from above,
like the gentle rain let the skies drop it down.

Let the earth open and salvation bud forth;
let justice also spring up!

In the second lesson we see Jesus as God incarnate administering justice and salvation in the form of healing. The handicapped mentioned in the text would be marginal people and many of their illnesses may have been caused by unjust distribution of wealth and wretched living conditions. Jesus, whom John the Baptist probably expected to be a mighty warrior or a powerful and authoritative prince, comes as mercy incarnate and shows his regal character through compassion. We cannot help but remember the words of Portia in *The Merchant of Venice:*

The quality of mercy is not strain'd,
It droppeth like the gentle dew from heaven
Upon the place beneath: it is twice bless'd;
It blesses him that gives and him that takes;
Tis mightiest in the mightiest; it becomes
The throned monarch better than his crown;
His scepter shows the force of temporal power,
The attribute to awe and majesty,
Wherein doth sit the dread and fear of kings;
But mercy is above the scepter's sway,
It is enthroned in the hearts of kings,
It is an attribute of God himself,
And earthly power doth then show likest God's
When mercy seasons justice . . .
That in the course of justice, none of us
Should see salvation: we do pray for mercy,
And that same prayer does teach us all to render
The deeds of mercy.   (Shakespeare, *Merchant,* 4.1)

Intercessions

That God's rich blessing may be upon those who administer justice;

That we may not waste God's earth.

Prayer

God, Impartial Judge of the Quick and the Dead,
we live in a most litigious world.
Teach us to deal gently with human error.
Let the dew of our mercy
nourish the fruits of the Spirit
in those hearts which have gone astray. Amen.

191 Thursday of the Third Week of Advent

Isa 54:1-10; Luke 7:24-30

The Niobe of nations! there she stands,
Childless and crownless, in her voiceless woe . . .
Yet freedom! yet thy banner, torn, but flying,
Streams like a thunderstorm against the wind.
(Byron, Childe Harold's Pilgrimage)

Como escuchase un llanto, me paré en el repecho
y me acerqué a la puerta del rancho del camino.
Un niño de ojos dulces me miró desde el lecho
¡y una ternura inmensa me embriagó como un vino!
(Gabriela Mistral, "El Niño Solo," Desolación, 8)

The Hebrew Scripture reading brings the good tidings of liberation to Israel in the Babylonian captivity. It is a poem of triumph and joy and expresses the liberation in terms of a woman who can bear and rear many children. This was the chief and most honourable function of most women in the ancient world. Before the development of belief in a full life after death people thought that children brought immortality to tribes and kingdoms. The second reading speaks of the Baptist and says that no one born of woman was greater than the Baptist: his mother, like the nation in exile, was barren, infertile. Her family's and neighbours' joy was exuberant when John was born (Lk 1:58). Owing to the providential circumstances of his conception and birth all wondered about the destiny of this child (Lk 1:65-66). "Was not the hand of the Lord upon him''? Yet each child, whether s/he will be famous or not, reflects most purely the image of God and the Kingdom of Christ.

Call home the child, whose credulous first hours
Burn at the heart of living, and surprise
The better reason with unbidden truth.

(David McCord, *A Bucket of Bees*)

Intercessions

For God's blessing upon those who have adopted children;

For us that we may not defeat God's plan.

Prayer

God, our Father and our Mother,
rekindle within us
an awe for the mystery of birth.
Find homes and love for those children
cast adrift on life's tempestuous wave
by indifferent parents. Amen.

192 Friday of the Third Week of Advent

Isa 56:1-3, 5-8; John 5:33-36

The kingdom of Heaven is thrown open to all eunuchs.

(Tertullian, *De Monogamia*)

Arbol de sangre moja la mañana
por donde gime la recién parida.
Su voz deja cristales en la herida
y un gráfico de hueso en la ventana. . . .

Pero otro Adán oscuro setá soñando
neutra luna de piedra sin semilla
donde el niño de luz se irá quemando.

(Federico García Lorca, ''Adan,'' *The Selected Poems of*
Federico García Lorca. New York: New Directions, 1961, 28)

The first lesson speaks of God's love for two classes of ostracized people in the ancient world. Firstly, there are the eunuchs. Deuteronomy 23:1 says, "He that is wounded in the stones, or hath his privy member cut off, shall not enter into the congregation of the Lord." These were men who were castrated, very often, because they served in courts where there were large harems: they often served as guards. But they were not regarded as real men and usually they could not become part of a religious community. The other class is the foreigner. Foreigners were not allowed in the part of the temple reserved for Jewish men (the women had a court of their own). Isaiah predicted a time when these people would be accepted into the religious community and he describes how God respected, honoured, loved and rewarded the religious observance which they were allowed to practice, e.g. in the home and on the sabbath. In Acts 8, Luke, obviously with this passage from Isaiah in mind, shows how the Christian missionaries went to the Samaritans, whom many people regarded as foreigners. Then he has a charming, quiet passage about the conversion of an Ethiopian eunuch who served as treasurer in the court of Queen Candace (Acts 8:26-40). He must have been a Jew or proselyte because he is reading a passage from Isa 53.

Intercessions

For those excluded from religious communities;

For Catholic women who are excluded from the ordained ministry.

Prayer

God, you did create man and woman,
  male and female,
    in your image and likeness.
      Help us not to mar this image
        by violent abuse
          or subtle cruelty. Amen.

10   Fourth Sunday of Advent
Cycle A

Isa 7:10-14; Rom 1:1-7; Matt 1:18-24

This is the month, and this the happy morn,
Wherein the Son of Heav'n's eternal King,
Of wedded maid and virgin mother born,
Our great redemption from above did bring,
or so the holy sages once did sing,
That He our deadly forfeit[1] should release,
And with His Father work us a perpetual peace.

(Milton, *On the Morning of Christ's Nativity*)

¡Porque yo sé que tengo tanto amor en los brazos!
Así me pesan, hondos, graves como la vida.
Un hijo o un amante o un ramo de jazmines,
o un retazo de viento o el talle de una amiga.

Aquí en los brazos siento gravitar las estrellas,
el pecho de Dios mismo, la dorada gavilla,
el vuelo de los pájaros, el corazón del mundo,
el peso inagotable de mi melancolía.

(Susanna March, "Amor," *Antologia*, 237)

In the great story of the Exodus of the children of Israel from Egypt women play essential roles. Firstly, the Hebrew midwives who saved the male children from Pharaoh's genocide; secondly, Moses' mother, who preserved his life; thirdly, his sister, who watched over the cradle of rushes and found a most appropriate wet nurse, that is, his own mother, for her brother; fourthly, the Egyptian princess who adopted and raised Moses; and fifthly, Miriam, the prophetess, who appears to have had an important role in the Exodus event and led the liturgical dance after the crossing of the Red Sea. Other women saviour figures arose in Israel, most notably, Deborah, judge and military strategist, Tamar, Rahab, Bathsheba, Esther and Judith. It is against this background that Ann Johnson in her book *Miryam of Nazareth* sets the story of Mary, the mother of Jesus. She uses the Hebrew form of her name, Miryam. She enters into the mentality of these women. She says:

In prayer Miryam watched.
Eyes of her soul turned inward, she watched.

[1]The sin of Adam and Eve and their expulsion from Paradise.

Ears of her spirit stretched out, she watched.
Watched for Yahweh in stillness.

In awe Miryam listened.
With the firm beat of her heart, she listened.
With the deep stroke of her breath, she listened.
Listened for Yahweh in stillness.

In the stillness Miryam reached out.
Mind alive, she reached out.
Memory reflecting, she reached out.
Inviting her God to inspire.

The Shadow streamed into her being.
Greeting the core of her soul.
Hearing she stretched for the life source.
Embracing the quickening call.

"How is this? I know not!" she responded.
Stumbling in God's desert of time.
"But you speak and all things come together.

I will
  as you say
    let it be."

Her lifetime of shadowy knowing it was
  confirmed in the quieting joy.
Summoning cadences, ancient and deep,
  echoed the call of God's peace.
> (Miryam of Nazareth: Woman of Strength and Wisdom,
> Notre Dame: Ave Maria Press, 1984.)

Women represent the "humble and lowly" (Zephaniah), the "low-born and despised" (Paul), and the "single-hearted" (Matthew), mentioned in our three readings.

Intercessions

For those to whom the world does not grant human dignity;

For a true realization of the beatitudes of Jesus.

Prayer

Holy Spirit, our Mother,
  you did speak to the attentive ear
    of your disciple, Mary.

Instill into us that potent power of listening
that we might redeem from weariness and loneliness
those battered by life's turbulence. Amen.

11 Fourth Sunday of Advent
Cycle B

2 Sam 7:1-5, 8-11, 16; Rom 16:25-27; Luke 1:26-38

The Lord showed me, so that I did see clearly, that he did not dwell in these temples which men had commanded and set up, but in people's hearts . . . his people were his temple, and he dwelt in them.

(George Fox, founder of the Society of Friends, *Journal*)

Si es María el mejor Templo
de Dios, cuando se dedica
Templo a Dios, no puede ser
sino en nombre de María.

(Sor Juana, *Obras*, 296)

The first reading tells of King David and his plans to build a temple for Yahweh. But God told Nathan, the prophet, that David should not build a house for the deity. Instead God would give to David a house in the sense of a dynasty that would last for ever. David in all humility accepted God's decision and it was left for his son, Solomon, to construct the temple. Indeed, God's promise was to be realized in a superlative way in Jesus, the son of Mary. There is some tradition among the chosen people that a leader bearing God's name and character, would come in the latter times. Here is a fragment from the Dead Sea Scrolls which is quite close to the words of Gabriel to Mary (Lk 1:35).

2 Samuel 7	4 Qumran 243	Luke 1:32-4
I will raise up your heir after you, sprung from your loins, and I will make his kingdom firm. It is he who shall build a house for my name. And I will	[But your son] 7 shall be great upon the earth, 8 [O King! All (men) shall] make [peace], and all shall serve 9 [him. He shall be called the son of]	Great will be his dignity and he will be called Son of the Most High. The Lord God will give him the throne of David his father. He will rule over

2 Samuel 7	4 Qumran 243	Luke 1:32-4
make his royal throne firm forever. I will be a father to him, and He shall be a son to me. . . . Your house and your kingdom shall endure forever before me; your throne shall stand firm forever.	the [G]reat [God], and by his name shall he be named. (Col ii). 1 He shall be hailed (as) the Son of God, and they shall call him Son of the Most High. As comets (flash) 2 to the sight, so shall be their kingdom. . . . (trans. Fitzmyer)	the house of Jacob forever and his reign will be without end. . . . The Holy Spirit shall come upon you and the power of the Most High will over-shadow you, hence the holy offspring to be born will be called Son of God.

A contemporary author places Mary in the context of the Exodus with other great heroes and heroines of the event:

> The work of Miryam was auspiciously begun.
> In the fullness of their years, it was this Levite family,
> Aaron, Miryam and Moses,
> who centered the Hebrew dream of freedom
> who announced the Hebrew intention to Pharaoh
> who accomplished the Hebrew exodus from Egypt.
> (Ann Johnson, Miryam of Nazareth, 59)

Intercessions

> That, like Mary, women may become potent mediators of salvation;
> That we may be adaptable to God's surprising will.

Prayer

> Mighty Forger of New and Uncharted Ways,
>   impell us with the fire of your Spirit.
>   Enable us to lay firm
>   the foundation stones of justice.
>   May your people
>   march in your glory
>   to everlasting peace.
>   Amen.

12 Fourth Sunday of Advent
Cycle C

Mic 5:1-4; Heb 10:5-10; Luke 1:39-45

A friend may well be reckoned the masterpiece of Nature.
(Ralph Waldo Emerson, *Friendship*)

He aquí que te anuncias.
Entre contradictorios ángeles te aproximas,
como una suave música te viertes,
como un vaso de aromas y de bálsamos. . . .
(Rosario Castellanos, "La Anunciación," *Poesia,* 34)

Pregnancy before betrothal was solemnized in marriage must have been a traumatic experience for Mary. She must have been subject to much criticism, especially when she would go to the public (village) well for water—surely a veritable gossiping centre. Her companions might mock and/or accuse her of unfaithfulness to her betrothed. Infidelity during an engagement was serious, for a bill of divorce was needed for breaking off a betrothal as well as a marriage. Her fellow women might have suggested that she was dabbling in magic if she spoke about a miraculous pregnancy. They might have advised an abortion. Mary went to Elizabeth and found one who believed in her. Elizabeth cried out with words very similar to those with which the elders praised Judith when she saved her country from destruction. Uzziah, one of the chief elders said:

> *Blessed are you, daughter, by the Most High God, above all the women on earth; and blessed be the Lord God, the creator of heaven and earth, who guided your blow at the head of the chief of our enemies. Your deed of hope will never be forgotten by those who tell of the might of God. May God make this redound to your everlasting honor, rewarding you with blessings, because you risked your life when your people were being oppressed, and you averted our disaster, walking uprightly before our God. And all the people answered. Amen! Amen!* (Jdt 13:18-20)

Judith had decapitated the leader of the enemy.

While we should not, perhaps, associate Mary with violence, it is hard to imagine that she was politically indifferent and she may well have sympathized with rebellious leaders in Palestine, e.g. the revolt against taxation by Judas the Galilean.

> *[They] maintained that this census would lead to nothing less than*
> *complete slavery, and they called upon the people to vindicate their*
> *liberty. They argued that, if they succeeded, they would enjoy the*
> *consequences of their good fortune, and if they failed, they would*
> *at least have the honour and glory of having shown a greatness*
> *of spirit. Moreover, God would surely assist them in their under-*
> *taking if, inspired by such ideals, they spared no effort to realize*
> *them.*   (Josephus, *Antiquities* 18:1-5)

This revolt arose in Galilee and took place very close to the date to which Luke assigns the birth of Jesus. Further, we know that many Jews were crucified in Galilee about this time. Could this be the explanation of Joseph and Mary fleeing for refuge to Egypt as Matthew reports? Against this background Mary appears as a strong woman not removed from the political arena.

Intercessions

> *That strong and just leaders may arise in turbulent countries;*
> *That we might find people whom we may trust.*

Prayer

> *Holy Spirit, Mother and Friend,*
> *spread the protective wings of your love*
> *over those men and women*
> *who have engendered children out of wedlock.*
> *May the wonder of new life*
> *alert them to their responsibilities.*
> *May the little one conceived*
> *be surrounded by love, find a place in society,*
> *and become a compassionate member of your kingdom. Amen.*

LAS POSADAS[2]

The *Posadas* are a Hispanic devotion commemorating Mary and Joseph seeking lodging in Bethlehem. These services are a means of preparation for Christmas in the villages of Latin America principally in Mexico. They are the novena in preparation for the feast of Christmas

---

[2] I have taken some of this material from *Fiestas Navideñas*, Patricio F. Florio, (San Antonio, Texas: Archdiocese of San Antonio, Office of Religious Education, 1981); but I have composed the prayers for each *posada* myself.

beginning on December 16 and ending on the 24 with the "Misa da Gallo" or the midnight mass.

"Las Posadas" is a word which is very well known in Mexico and the Southwest of the United States. It signifies "shelter," "protection," "welcome." It has always been a custom to fill the celebration of the *Posadas* with joy and song.

It is thought that the *Posadas* owe their origin to Brother Diego de Soria, a religious of the Order of St. Augustine. This enthusiastic priest introduced this devotion in Mexico in the church of Alcomán in 1587. He hoped to counteract the celebrations of the Aztecs in honour of the god of war, Huitzlopochtli. The *Posadas* took place precisely within the period of Christmas and was a strong attraction for the new Christians. The *Posadas* of Brother Diego became so popular that they immediately spread to other churches of Mexico and of the neighbouring countries. Later they began to be celebrated in the individual houses.

In these celebrations the "pilgrims" go from house to house guided by an angel who leads the donkey on which the Virgin is seated. At her side is Saint Joseph. One can procure statues of Joseph leading the donkey. During the procession the statues are carried on the shoulders of the walkers.

The order of the services is as follows:

1. Altar preparation. The altar where the holy travellers are is an integral part of the *Posadas*.

2. Greeting and song.

3. Reading of Scripture.

4. Community prayer in which petitions are offered for the necessities of the community, of the universal Church and of the whole world.

5. Procession. During the procession the litany of Mary is sung.

6. From the church where the prayers have been offered one procedes to the house whose turn it is to receive the travellers. An acolyte goes ahead with the cross. The others follow with lighted lamps and candles. At the end they carry the statues of Mary and Joseph (*las andas*).

The people forming the procession ask for *posada*, they knock on the doors of the neighbors, who deny them *posada*, and eventually they reach the house where they are going to celebrate *Las Posadas*. There they are received, offer prayer and enjoy refreshments.

194 December 17[3]
Posada II

Gen 49:2, 8-10; Matt 1:1-17

. . . This nurse, this teeming womb of royal kings,
Fear'ed by their breed and famous by their birth.

(Shakespeare, *Richard II*, 2.1.40)

Hoy, que el Mayor de los Reyes
llega del Mundo a las puertas,
a todos sus pretendientes
ha resuelto dar Audiencia.

Atended: porque hoy, a todos,
los memoriales decreta,
y a su Portal privilegios
concede de covachuela.

(Sor Juana, *Obras*, 263)

Although the above English quotation refers to England *per se*, it expresses a sentiment experienced by both men and women concerning their homeland and pedigree. The first Scripture lesson predicts the political ascendancy of Judah and the second traces Jesus' genealogy back to Abraham. Biblical and ancient genealogies are works of art: they are not precise historically and should not be taken literally. Here Matthew wishes to trace Jesus' birth back to the great patriarch, Abraham, and his wife, Sarah. Among the Jewish people genealogies were important for kings, priests and sometimes military figures. Luke records Jesus' genealogy after his baptism and traces it back to Adam (and Eve)!

But kingly lineage brings responsibilities which far outweigh the prestige and ceremony of sovereignty. We may take, for example, the words of Henry V before the battle of Agincourt.

What infinite heart's ease must kings neglect,
That private men enjoy?
And what have kings that privates have not too,
Save ceremony, save general ceremony?
And what art thou, thou idol ceremony?
What kind of god art though, that suffer'st more
Of mortal griefs than do thy worshippers?

[3]The lectionary does not provide readings for December 16.

What are thy rents? what are thy comings-in?
O ceremony, show me but thy worth! . . .

I am a king that find thee; and I know,
Tis not the balm, the sceptre, and the ball,
The sword, the mace, the crown imperial,
The inter-tissued robe of gold and pearl,
The farcèd title running 'fore the king,
The throne he sits on nor the tide of pomp
That beats upon the high shore of this world:
No, not all these thrice-gorgeous ceremony,
Not all these, laid in bed majestical,
Can sleep so soundly as the wretched slave. . . .

(Shakespeare, Henry V, 4.1.233–241, 256–265)

Greeting

Sisters and brothers, let us greet each other as equals and with love for we are fellow priests, prophets and monarchs in the Christian community.

Intercession

That our compassion may embrace all unmarried parents and help to relieve their anxieties;

That we may show sympathy to all who travel in foreign environments, especially the immigrants from Latin America.

Prayer

God, our Monarch and our Servant,
you have called all to various vocations
in church and state.
We are all kings, priests and prophets
through baptism.
Grant through your Son, who so deftly interwove
humanity and divinity,
that we, his brothers and sisters,
may discern with joy
the contribution of all individuals
to our society and to your kingdom. Amen.

Dismissal

Go in peace,
with a heart open to all.

195 December 18
Posada III

Jer 23:5-8; Matt 1:18-24

Marriage is the hospital of love. (German Proverb)

Why that the naked, poor, and mangled peace,
Dear nurse of arts, plenties, and joyful births,
Should not in this best garden of the world,
Our fertile France, put up her lovely visage?
(Shakespeare, *Henry V,* 5.2.34–37)

Divino José: si son
vuestras glorias tan inmensas,
que ignorándolas ninguno,
no hay alguno que las sepa

—pues aunque es notoria a todos
vuestra Dignitad suprema,
se sabe que es grande, pero
no se mide su grandeza—. (Sor Juana, *Obras,* 270)

The first lesson speaks of a monarch who will bring prosperity and security to the nation. His is a peace which is founded only upon justice and liberation. The second lesson shows Joseph, the betrothed of Mary, going beyond the law and his marital rights to avoid domestic violence and to give safety, home and shelter from slander for his betrothed and her child. Joseph could have followed the law which says:

> *When a man, after marrying a woman and having relations with*
> *her, is later displeased with her because he finds in her something*
> *indecent, and therefore he writes out a bill of divorce and hands*
> *it to her, thus dismissing her from his house. If on leaving his*
> *house she goes and becomes the wife of another man, and the sec-*
> *ond husband, too, comes to dislike her and dismisses her from his*
> *house by handing her a written bill of divorce; or if this second*
> *man who has married her, dies; then her former husband, who*
> *dismissed her, may not again take her as his wife after she has*
> *become defiled.* (Deut 24:1)

Joseph shows himself as a man of compassion, not seeking redress by litigation but forming a bond of loving kindness with Mary and the child within her. If, as tradition claims, the couple did refrain from sexual intercourse after the birth of Jesus then this would be a decision on the part of Joseph, not Mary, who would have no power to do so. As an observant Jew Joseph might have felt that he should not cohabit with a woman who had born another person's child, even a child conceived miraculously. This would be on the same principle as the divorced woman in the Scripture passage above. Joseph's was a marriage of benevolence.

George Pettie speaks of marriage as such:

> Amongst all the bonds of benevolence, and goodwill there is none more honorable, ancient or honest than marriage.
>
> (George Pettie, *Petite Palace of Pettie His Pleasure*)

Or the words of our own marriage service might describe Joseph's disposition: "To have and to hold from this day forward, for better, for worse, for richer, for poorer, in sickness and in health, to love and to cherish, till death us do part" (*Book of Common Prayer*).

Greeting

> Sisters and Brothers, let us greet each other with that singleness of heart and compassion that Joseph showed to Mary.

Intercessions

> That men may acknowledge paternity and accept responsibility for their children;
>
> That there may be an end to domestic violence.

Prayer

> God, Spouse of your chosen people,
>   you remain faithful
>   in the face of all our infidelities.
> Let all earthly spouses
>   drink deeply of your covenant love.
> May cherishing love,
>   understanding, innocent of all suspicion,
>   and patient fortitude
>   flow through the hearts of all
>   united in the sacred bond of marriage.
> May they be sacrosanct one to another.
>   Amen.

Dismissal

Go, anointed by God with healing love.

196   December 19
Posada IV

Jdgs 13:2-7, 24-25; Luke 1:5-25

Posada 4

To live a barren sister all your life,
Chanting faint hymns to the cold fruitless moon.
(Shakespeare, *Midsummer Night's Dream*, 1.1.72)

THESE
are the desolate, dark weeks
when nature in its barrenness
equals the stupidity of man.

The year plunges into night
and the heart plunges
lower than night.   (W. C. Williams, *These*)

La mujer que no mece a un hijo en el regazo,
cuyo calor y aroma alcance a sus entrañas,
tiene una laxitud de mundo entre los brazos;
todo su corazón congoja inmensa baña.
(Gabriela Mistral, "La Mujer Esteril," *Desolación*, 8)

As procreation, especially of a male child, was considered the greatest blessing which God could bestow upon men and women, barrenness was seen as a curse or chastisement (cf. Lev 20:20-21 and Jer 22:30). Genesis 30: 1 says that Rachel preferred death to sterility. Jewish maxims reflect this same sentiment: to lack children is like death (*Nedarim* 64b); a childless man should not be a member of the Sanhedrin (*Sanhedrin* 36b); a husband should divorce his wife if she does not produce a child within ten years (*Yebamot* 66). There is a Jewish legend which tells of a happy couple who were married for ten years but had no children. So they were advised to separate and the man to take another wife. The Rabbi told them to end their marriage with a feast just as they had begun it with a feast. During the meal the husband requested the wife to take from the house the thing she loved most. Consequently, she plied her husband with wine until he fell asleep. Then she bade the servants to carry him to her new house. When he awoke he was amazed to find himself in the home of his former wife. When he asked the reason for this the wife replied: "'But you told me to take away my most precious possession.''

Greeting

Brothers and sisters, let us greet each other with joy and mutually call to mind the most precious possessions which God has given us.

Intercessions

For all who long for children that God will bless them as he blessed Hannah, Mary and Elizabeth;

For all those who have lost children by death, separation, or political "disappearance" especially. . . .

Prayer

God of Infinite Surprise,
  You caused barren men and women,
    to rejoice in offspring.
Visit our minds and our souls
  that they, too, may become fertile
    to replenish the world with beauty.
      Amen.

Dismissal

Go—to bear fruits of bounteous service to others.

197 December 20
Posada V

Isa 7:10-14; Luke 1:26-38

The Divine Paradox

A God and yet a man?
A Maid and yet a Mother?
Wit wonders what wit can
Conceive this or the other.

A God, and can He die?
A dead man, can He live?
What wit can well reply?
What reason Reason give?

God, truth itself, doth teach it.
Man's wit sinks too far under
By reason's power to reach it.
Believe, and leave to wonder.

(R. S. Loomis and R. Willard, *Medieval English Verse*
and Prose in Modernized Versions, New York:
Appleton-Century-Crofts, 1948)

Niño Dios, que lloras naciendo:
perlas y flechas tus lágrimas son;
con las perlas redimes mis culpas,
con las flechas me hieres de amor.   (Sor Juana, *Obras*, 330)

Isaiah portrays God giving a sign to Ahaz. The prophet, of course, did not have the conception of Jesus by Mary in mind but Christians soon read back into the text a prediction of Mary's mysterious pregnancy. We cannot fathom the depth of this mystery but it is sufficient to reflect that God does not always function as we do and our logical minds cannot always understand the thoughts and plans of God. The best we can do is to live open to mystery and paradox. Thus our lives will not be prosaic but full of poetry and power.

Greeting

Sisters and brothers, let us greet each other and rejoice to see within
each individual the image of the creator, full of paradox, mystery
and challenge.

Intercession

That we may be able to accept the illogical and unexpected things
in life;

For a greater understanding of those who do not conform to social
or religious norms.

Prayer

God, our Mother,
you cradled Salvation
in a woman's womb,
surrounding him with rich warmth
in that still darkness.
Show us that eternal life comes not
through fear of Hell
but through the nurture
carried by woman's blood.
Amen.

Dismissal

Go, men and women, to nurture the world.

198   December 21
Posada VI

Cant 2:8-14; or Zeph 3:14-18; Luke 1:39-45

This heaven of beauty . . . . (Shakespeare, *Henry VIII*, 1.4.60)

Y extasiada murmuro:
—Cuerpo mío: ¡estás hecho
de substancia inmortal!
   (Juana de Ibarbourou, "Carne Inmortal," *Once Grandes*, 250)

The above English quotation comes from Wolsey as he looks at the fair
young ladies attending a ball. His remark is not trivial. The supernatural
nature of human love is vividly portrayed in the Bible in the Song of
Solomon and in the various commentaries which have been written on
it down through the ages. This biblical book is a collection of love songs,
very erotic in nature, which have been interpreted by our Jewish

brothers and sisters as the covenant love relationship between God and Israel and by the Christian community as the union between Christ and the Church. It is a fitting symbol of the wedding of our mortal humanity to the essence of the immortal Godhead so that it celebrates the very essence of Christmas. In this feast we see the innate attraction of Godhood for humanhood.

The core of the incarnation is friendship between God and humankind. We see a foreshadowing of this in the mutual love between David and Jonathan:

> . . . Jonathan had become as fond of David as if his life depended on him; he loved him as he loved himself. Saul laid claim to David that day and did not allow him to return to his father's house. And Jonathan entered into a bond (covenant) with David, because he loved him as himself. Jonathan divested himself of the mantle he was wearing and gave it to David, along with his military dress, and his sword, his bow and his belt. David then carried out successfully every mission on which Saul sent him.
>
> (1 Sam 18:1-5)

In ancient times clothing was regarded as part of one's personality. So Jonathan's vesting of David meant that he shared his personality with him. In that strength David went from victory to victory. But the clothing that Jesus took in the incarnation was not the outer vesture but the very flesh and body of humanity, man and woman. Cicero, the great Roman orator, says, "A friend is, as it were, a second self" (*De Amicitia*). We might say that humanity is a "second self" to God. Here are two more reflections on friendship.

> Time draweth wrinkles in a fair face, but addeth fresh colors to a fast friend, which neither heart, nor cold, nor misery, nor place, nor destiny can alter or diminish.   (John Lyly, *Endymion*)

> A true friend unbosums freely, advises justly, assists readily, adventures boldly, takes all patiently, defends courageously, and continues a friend unchangeably.
>
> (William Penn: *Some Fruits of Solitude*)

Greeting

> Sisters and brothers, let us greet each other with the covenant love of friendship and pray that an international covenant of peace may be implemented in our days.

Intercessions

That sexual love may be reverenced and love between marriage part-
ners may be sanctified and enriched;

That our Christian people and all peoples may not enter the mar-
riage bond without sincere preparation and an honest desire to
bring their nuptial love to fruition both in times of difficulty and
times of joy.

Prayer

God of Constant Friendship,
we pray for the friendless of this world.
Let your Spirit, the begetter of all right relationships,
nurture a bond between them and their neighbors.
that the Lord may become Incarnate in them.
Amen.

Dismissal

Go, to make friends of God and humankind.

199   December 22
Posada VII

1 Sam 1:24-28; Luke 1:45-56

This royal infant (Heaven still move about her!)
Though in her cradle, yet now promises
Upon this land a thousand thousand blessings,
Which time shall bring to ripeness.

(Shakespeare, *Henry VIII*, 5.4)

Por humilde me exaltas. Tu mirada
benévola, transforma
mis llagas en ardientes esplendores.
He aquí que te acercas y me encuentras
rodeada de plegarias como de hogueras altas.

(Rosario Castellanos, "La Anunciación," *Poesia*, 34)

The Magnificat is not a pious or pietistic prayer offered by Mary but
rather a triumphant, revolutionary hymn predicting social equality for

all. It has its parallels in the fervent hymns and prayers offered by the Maccabees, Jewish men and women who fought against the persecutor of the Jews, Antiochus Epiphanes, in the second century before Christ. It is also similar to the hymns found among the Dead Sea Scrolls especially those in the *War Scroll between the Sons of Light against the Sons of Darkness*. This is a war manual describing the battle between the faithful and God on the one side and Satan and wicked men on the other. Mary is, therefore, presented as a politically minded, if not active, woman according to the culture of her time. Here is a modern version of the Magnificat.

The Magnificat

With pride and dignity I sing my song of joy when I feel the Lord's presence;

I am poor and very ordinary, but one day the Lord looked upon me
And the history of the poor will give witness to my joy.

God is unfettered and unpredictable, He is called our great friend.

And throughout our history He has favored those of us who are weak.

His triumphant force shows itself each day when He exposes the foolishness of the powerful.

He uncovers the feet of clay of those in power, and nourishes the yearning of the poor.

To those who come hungry He gives bread and wine.

And to the wealthy He exposes their selfishness and the emptiness of their ways.

This is God's desire: always to favor the poor.

Now finally we can walk.

He is faithful to His promises.

(By a Chilean woman, source unknown)

Greeting

Brothers and sisters, let us greet each other and, as we do so, remember all the oppressed in the world who need good cheer and encouragement.

Intercessions

For God's guidance and blessing for all socially and religiously concerned women, especially in Latin America, the Arab countries and India;

For the hungry, the homeless, the bereaved, the unlettered and the bewildered.

Prayer

God, *True Bulwark of the Oppressed,*
  you set your laws concerning the poor
    within the heart of the Sinai Covenant.
  Teach us to walk hand in hand
    with Mother Justice,
  mindful of the needs of the rich
    as well as the poor.
      Amen.

Dismissal

Go, march with justice,
  console the afflicted,
    win understanding with the comfortable.

200   December 23
Posada VIII

Mal 3:1-4; 23-24; Luke 1:57-66

Since you are tongue-tied, and so loth to speak,
In dumb significants proclaim your thoughts. . . .
                    (Shakespeare, *Henry VI* 2.4)

¡Oh Psiquis, oh mi alma: suena a són
moderno, a són de selva, a són de orgía
y a són marino, el són del corazón!
            (Ramon López Velarde, "El Són del Corazón,"
                    Anthology of Spanish Poetry, 147)

John the Baptist was the precursor of Jesus. Many thought of him as Elijah come to life again and even others that he was the Coming One, the Messiah. His conception and birth were surrounded by mystery. The first lesson about God's messenger coming to the temple is appropriate because the father of John the Baptist, Zechariah, received Gabriel's news of his wife's future conception while he was ministering in the temple. Luke tells us that Zechariah was struck dumb. Whether he suffered a stroke or Luke is speaking symbolically we shall never know but the struggles of the aphasic (mute) are brought to our attention here. In one of the most bloody plays of Shakespeare there is a profoundly moving passage: it is of a father addressing his daughter, who has been mutilated and has no tongue for speech.

Speechless complainer, I will learn thy thought;
In thy dumb action will I be as perfect
As begging hermits in their holy prayers:
Thou shalt not sigh, nor hold thy stumps to heaven,
Nor wink, nor nod, nor kneel, nor make a sign.

But I, of these, will wrest an alphabet,
And by still practice, learn to know thy meaning.
(Shakespeare, *Titus Andronicus*, 3.2)

Greeting

Brothers and sisters, let us greet each other using God's special gift of speech.

Intercessions

For all those who have never had the joy of hearing music or poetry or the ordinary kindly words of their families and friends.

For ourselves that we may gain greater understanding of nonverbal communication;

For those who are unable to speak.

Prayer

God our Creator,
your wise Spirit played at the creation of the world
and delighted in the children of humanity.
Grant us the grace of play and leisure,
that in this "busy beat of time"
we may glimpse your timelessness and your cheer. Amen.

Dismissal

Go in peace
to treasure eye, ear and tongue.

201 December 24
Posada IX

2 Sam 7:1-5, 8-11, 16; Luke 1:67-79

A peace above all earthly dignities,
A still and quiet conscience.   (Shakespeare, *Henry VIII*, 3.2.380)

. . .

Esta ardua criatura
sapiente y tan desierta entre sus albas
anclada está en la dócil paz oscura
de su casa.

(Juana de Iarbourou, "Pax," *Once Grandes*, 265)

In today's reading Luke presents Zechariah uttering a prediction after the recovery of his speech. It is a hymn of praise of God's faithfulness and covenant love shown particularly in freeing the Hebrews from their servitude and enemies. Zechariah and Elizabeth's son is to prepare the way for God's Coming One so that people may walk in peace.

> *. . . I demand . . .*
> *Why that the naked, poor, and mangled peace,*
> *Dear nurse of arts, plenties and joyful births,*
> *Should not, in this best garden of the world,*
> *Our fertile France, put up her lovely visage?*
> *Alas! she hath from France too long been chased;*
> *And all her husbandry doth lie on heaps,*
> *Corrupting its own fertility . . .*
> *Even so our houses, and ourselves, and children,*
> *Have lost, or do not learn, for want of time,*
> *The sciences that should become our country . . .*
> * and my speech entreats*
> *That I may know the let, why gentle peace*
> *Should not expel these inconveniences,*
> *And bless us with her former qualities.*

(Shakespeare, *Henry V*, 5.2.32–40, 56–58, 64–67)

Greeting

Sisters and brothers, let us greet each other with profound peace.

Intercessions

For peace in the Holy Land;

*For our homes, that they may become havens of peace to us and
to all who call upon our hospitality.*

Prayer

*God of Poetry and Story,
  grant us "fertile peace."
May we nourish those arts
  which cultivate sensitivity and human refinement
in the hearts of all men and women. Amen.*

Dismissal

*Go in peace,
  to be educated by the poor and powerless.*

13   December 25
Christmas Day
The Vigil

Isa 62:1-5; Acts 13:16-17, 22-25; Matt 1:1-25, or 1:18-25

*To sit alone in the lamplight with a book spread out before you,
and hold intimate converse with men of unseen generations—such
is a pleasure beyond compare.*

> (Y. Kenko, *Essays on Idleness,* trans. D. Keene,
> *Anthology of Japanese Literature,* New York: Grove Press, 1955)

*Débil mujer, pobre mujer que entiende,
dolor de siglos conocí al beberlo:
Oh, el alma mía soportar no puede
todo su peso.*

> (Alfonsina Storni, "Peso Ancestral," *Once Grandes,* 295)

The Bible is the memory (or memories) of a covenant community,
the message of God passed down from generation to generation. It
is reflected upon, honed down, elaborated, never static, subject to the
novelty of the Spirit who pervades the human community. On the vigil

of Christmas we are presented in the first reading with the joyful union between God and the bride, Israel: it is expressed in exuberant poetry. However, the third lesson presents a rather prosaic genealogy. But a genealogy need not be dull. Biblical genealogies are not scientific, "accurate" in our sense of the word. They are works of art which provide a bridge over gaps in history and the correct pedigree for leaders, military, political, or religious. Of note in Matthew's genealogy is the unusual inclusion of four women. They are: Tamar (Gen 38) who "tricked" her father-in-law into fulfilling the law and providing her with a son; Rahab, a prostitute, who protected the Hebrew spies in the city of Jericho; Ruth who, after the death of her husband, went beyond the law and took the initiative in allying herself with Boaz, her late husband's kin, and thus raising up children to her deceased husband; and Bathsheba whom David took in adultery and who became the mother of the majestic King Solomon.

All these women went beyond the call of duty and became important links in the pedigree of Jesus and, in a way, they foreshadow Mary. In a mystical Jewish work called the *Zohar*, Tamar is said to have possessed the gift of prophecy and to have determined to fulfill her role as an ancestress of the Davidic Messiah (*Zohar* Gen 188ab). BathSheba is numbered among the twenty-two women of valor (*Midrash Hagadol* to Gen 23:1). Ruth was seen as an archetype of the righteous convert. People saw in her name "one who saturated the Holy One, blessed be He, with songs and hymns" (*Berakhot* 7b); or one who considered well (*ra'atah*) the words of her mother-in-law (*Ruth Rabbah* 2:9). In Jewish folklore Rahab converted to Judaism, married Joshua, and became the ancestress of eight prophets, including Jeremiah, and one prophetess, Hulda (*Megillah* 14b). Thus Matthew in the pedigree of Jesus has thrown into high relief four "forgotten" women.

Intercessions

> For forgotten women, past and present;
> For a deeper understanding of Scripture.

Prayer

> Creator God, you made man and woman
> in your own image and likeness.
> Make us sensitive to the role of women
> in salvation history. Amen.

14 Mass at Midnight

Isa 9:1-6; Titus 2:11-14; Luke 1:1-14

The first reading appears to be either an ode celebrating a coronation or a birthday, probably of King Hezekiah. To celebrate a birthday is to celebrate one's election by God. This ode speaks of the leader's character and kingdom in highly laudatory terms and forms a contrast to the uncelebrated birth of Jesus, whose importance is only revealed through the words of the angel to the shepherds. Yet it is entirely appropriate that Luke should present shepherds receiving the message. In the ancient world "shepherd" was a synonym for "king" or "leader." For example, a Greek philosopher called Dio Chrysostom, who wrote four discourses on kingship, speaks thus of the duties of a king: the king is called the shepherd of the peoples: "For the shepherd's business is simply to oversee, guard, and protect the flocks, not by heavens, to slaughter, butcher, and skin them . . . ."

David, too, was a shepherd. A psalm from the Dead Sea Scrolls speaks beautifully of God's calling David. He appeared insignificant beside his brothers but God looked into his heart.

A Hallelujah of David the Son of Jesse

Smaller was I than my brothers
  and the youngest of the sons of my father,
So he made me shepherd of his flock
  and ruler over his kids.

My hands have made an instrument
  and my fingers a lyre;
And [so] have I rendered glory to the Lord,
  thought I, within my soul.

The mountains do not witness to him,
  nor do the hills proclaim;
The trees have cherished my words
  and the flock my works.

For who can proclaim and who can bespeak
  and who can recount the deeds of the Lord?
Everything has God seen,
  every thing has he heard and he has heeded.

He sent his prophet to anoint me,
  Samuel to make me great;
My brothers went out to meet him,
  handsome of figure and appearance.

> Though they were tall of stature,
>   and handsome by their hair,
> The Lord God chose them not.
>
> But he sent and took me from behind the flock
>   and anointed me with holy oil;
> And he made me leader of his people
>   and ruler over the sons of his covenant.
>
> (Discoveries of the Judean Desert 4:55–56)

> . . . toqué, el cuerpo de un niño, yo quería
> pedirle ver y me encontré mirando. . . .
>
> (Luis Rosales, Del Pastor Ciego, Antologia, 83)

Intercessions

> For children born in prisons, without shelter, without love;
>
> For wise and selfless leaders.

Prayer

> O God, our creator and preserver,
>   speak to our untutored hearts.
> Teach us the futility of war and strife,
>   defence and counter-defence.
> Show us that the only weapons which will bring peace are
>   fraternal and sororal love,
> justice and humility. Amen

15 Mass at Dawn

> "Rabbi Jose bar Hanina taught: In the whole world you find no
> occupation more despised than the shepherd, who all his days walks
> about with his staff and his pouch. Yet David presumed to call
> the Holy One, blessed be he, a shepherd!"
>
> (Midrash on Psalms, trans. Braude)

> Corderito mio,
> suavidad callada:
> mi pecho es tu gruta
> de musgo afelpada.
>
> (Gabriela Mistral, Corderito)

This Mass is known as the Shepherd's Mass. Although in the Ancient Near East "shepherd" was a common title for "ruler," in New Testament times the average shepherd belonged to the fringes of society. In his presentation of the revelation made to the shepherds and their hasty response to come to acknowledge the Savior, Luke may recall the stories of Moses and David. After his flight from Egypt, Moses tended the sheep of his father-in-law. It was there that he received his revelation in the burning bush and that he was commissioned by God to lead the Chosen people from Israel. It was also there that he was told the "Name" of God, that is, was granted a special insight into the being of the deity. Similarly, David was caring for sheep when Samuel came seeking the future king of Israel and was called from the flock to be anointed. According to Luke the shepherds (and shepherdesses) are the first to receive the Good News of the arrival of the Messiah.

Intercessions

That God may come to the "little" people;

That we may recognize and accept God's coming.

Prayer

Good and caring Shepherd,
you called Abraham and Sarah,
Isaac and Rebecca,
Jacob and Rachel,
Moses and David
to be good shepherds of your people.
Grant that we might walk
worthily in their footsteps. Amen.

16 Mass during the Day

For she is a breath of the power of God,
a pure emanation of the glory of the Almighty;
therefore nothing defiled gains entrance into her.
For she is a reflection of eternal light,
a spotless mirror of the working of God,
and an image of his goodness.   (Wisdom of Solomon, 7:25-26)

Tengo miedo, miedo a no sé qué, el miedo de una visión confusa.
(Rafael Arévalo Martínez, *Oración*)

The Christmas celebration up to this point has emphasized the humanity of Jesus, the babe born of Mary. However, in this Mass the whole emphasis is upon the divinity of Jesus. The Epistle to the Hebrews speaks of God preparing his people through the prophets and finally sending his Son. The Prologue to John's Gospel speaks about the pre-existence of the Word. Both Hebrews and the Gospel of John draw from the wisdom literature of the Hebrew and Greek scriptures where Wisdom is seen as feminine, the feminine aspect of the deity. There she also is described as existing before creation and being God's mistress craftswoman. So our Mass today celebrates both the rich feminine and the rich masculine tradition about the deity. It presents Jesus, like Wisdom, as the image of God. He becomes incarnate that our being made in the image and likeness of God may be fully restored.

Intercessions

For a deeper appreciation of new models for God;
For all who are disciples of Lady Wisdom.

Prayer

God, gender-full and incomprehensible,
lead us on and on
to new revelations of your Personhood.
Let us not be brooked by fear or ridicule
but tread new paths with courageous march. Amen.

17 Sunday in the Octave of Christmas
The Holy Family
Cycles A, B and C

Sir 3:2-6, 12-14; Col 3:12-21

A. Matt 2:13-15, 19-23

The sea rocks her thousands of waves.
The sea is divine.
Hearing the loving sea
I rock my son.

The wind wandering by night
rocks the wheat.
Hearing the loving wind
I rock my son.

God, the Father, soundlessly rocks
His thousands of worlds.
Feeling His hand in the shadow
I rock my son.

(Gabriela Mistral, "Meciendo," trans. Doris Dana, in
Selected Poems of Gabriela Mistral, Baltimore:
John Hopkins Press, 1971, 43)

El mar sus millares de olas
mece, divino.
Oyendo a los mares amantes,
mezo a mí niño.
. . .
Dios Padre sus miles de mundos
mece sín ruido.
Sintiendo su mano en la sombra
mezo a mi niño.

(Gabriela Mistral, "Meciendo," *Selected Poems*, 42)

Although many scholars would view Matthew's infancy narratives as "pious fiction," there is certainly sufficient evidence that Herod the Great's reign was a blood bath. When he came into power he slew forty-five members of the Sanhedrin, the highest court of the Jewish people. Further, during his sovereignty he committed many dynastic murders including killing members of his own family. Herod's brutality increased towards the end of his reign. So it is possible that Joseph and Mary were among the various "refugees" many of whom over the centuries fled to Egypt. Another poem from Gabriel Mistral might illustrate the mind of Mary:

> When I am singing to you
> on earth all evil ends:
> as smooth as your forehead
> are the gulch and the bramble.
> When I am singing to you,
> for me all cruel things end:
> as gentle as your eyelids
> the lion and the jackal.
>
> (Gabriela Mistral, "Meciendo," *Selected Poems*, 71)

Intercessions

> For those afflicted, storm-tossed and bewildered;
>
> For the comfortable, the complacent and the indifferent.

Prayer

> God of Cherishing Love,
>   you taught Israel to walk,
> you held her in your arms,
>   you drew her with human cords, with bonds of love.
> You raised her to your cheek,
>   fed her and healed her.
> Do likewise for your Church
>   and teach us to show, not inflexibility, but love. Amen.

B. Luke 2:22-40

> Care keeps his watch in every old man's eye,
> And where care lodges, sleep will never lie.
>
> (Shakespeare, *Romeo and Juliet*, 2.3.35)

> ¡Qué descansada vida
> la del que huye el mundanal ruido,
> y sigue la escondida
> senda por donde han ido
> los pocos sabios que en el mundo han sido!
>
> (Fray Luis De León, "Vida Retirada,"
> *Penguin Book of Spanish Verse*, 431)

In typical Lukan style, the gospel lesson tells us of two "senior citizens" waiting for the consolation of Israel. They are both depicted as wise persons endowed with prophecy. Both in Hebrew and in Greco-Roman tradition old age was revered rather than lamented. Shakespeare claims that "honour, love, obedience, troops of friends," should accompany old age (*Macbeth*, 5.3). Further, Cicero in his eloquent treatise on old age says:

> *Give me a young man in whom there is something of the old, and an old man with something of the young: guided so, a man may grow old in body, but never in mind.* (Cicero, *De Senectute*)

Intercessions

> *For the eagerness of youth;*
> *For the wisdom of the aged.*

Prayer

> *God of Eternal Agelessness,*
>   *send a spirit of youth*
> *into those who have come of age.*
>   *Cherish their faculties*
> *by the creative power of your Spirit.*
>   *With memory undimmed,*
> *with mind alert*
>   *and tenderness in their hearts,*
> *let them find a place of expectant hope*
>   *within our communities. Amen.*

C. Luke 2:41-52

> *Who well lives, long lives; for this age of ours*
> *Should not be numbered by years, days, and hours.*
>   (Du Bartas, *Divine Weeks and Works*)

> *¡Ay, que llora Jesús!*
> *¡Tened, tened, que llora*
> *a los blandos arrullos*
> *de su Paloma!*

> *¡Tened, que tiembla;*
> *tened, que llora*
> *al rigor de la escarcha*
> *la misma Gloria!*   (Sor Juana Iñez, *Obra*, 342)

The lesson above spoke of old age but here we see Jesus as a teenager absorbed in intellectual inquiry. It is a lovely scene, one which we find only in Luke's Gospel. It cannot be historically verified. However, Luke's point is clear. Jesus seeks wisdom and also surmises his vocation from his Father. Later he must face the disillusion of this bright hope and be confronted with suffering, degradation and death. This experience is aptly expressed in the well-known poem by Wordsworth.

Our birth is but a sleep and a forgetting:
The Soul that rises with us, our life's Star,
  Hath had elsewhere its setting,
  And cometh from afar:
Not in entire forgetfulness,
And not in utter nakedness,
  But trailing clouds of glory do we come
  From God, who is our home:
Heaven lies about us in our infancy!

Shades of the prison-house begin to close
  Upon the growing Boy,
But He beholds the light, and whence it flows,
  He sees it in his joy;
The Youth, who daily farther from the east
  Must travel, still is Nature's Priest,
And by the vision splendid
  Is on his way attended;
At length the Man perceives it die away,
And fade into the light of common day.
              (W. Wordsworth, *Ode, Intimations of Immortality from*
                            Recollections of Early Childhood)

Intercessions

For the buoyant hope of youth;

For the fortitude of man- and woman-hood.

Prayer

Compassionate One,
  you gave your disciples a glimpse of hope and glory
in the transfiguration of your Son.
  In days of darkness and gloom
teach us to remember
  the hope of youth
and our divine origin in you. Amen.

203 Dec 29 Fifth Day in the Octave of Christmas

1 John 2:3-11 and Luke 2:22-35

He said likewise
That a lie which is half a truth is ever the blackest of lies,
That a lie which is all a lie may be met and fought with outright,
But a lie which is part truth is a harder matter to fight.
                                    (Tennyson, *The Grandmother*)

No tuve amor a las palabras;
si las usé con desnudez, si sufrí en esa busca,
fue por necesidad de no perder la vida,
y envejecer con algo de memoria
y alguna claridad.
        (Francisco Brines, "El por qué de las Palabras," *Recent Poetry*, 248)

In the moving Cuban film *La Ultima Cena (The Last Supper)*, which takes place in the eighteenth century, a slave master washes the feet of twelve African slaves and then invites them as guests for a great feast on Holy Thursday. Although the slave master might have been sincere, during his after dinner speech he justifies the institution of slavery, the physical punishment of slaves and he claims that their perfect happiness consists in bearing their fate with joy in imitation of Jesus. One slave, a former king in Africa, tells a very interesting story, in fact, a parable. He personifies the Truth and the Lie. Truth is the stronger and attractive character and all the people become his followers. Taking pity on the Lie the people give him weapons. With these he decapitates Truth. Truth groping about without eyes accidently wrenches off the head of the Lie and puts it on his own shoulders. From thence onwards Truth walks the earth with his own body but with the head of the Lie. With striking symbolic gesture the Slave-King lifts up a pig's head. There is, perhaps, no single meaning to this parable but one interpretation could be that Truth travels through the world disguised as the Lie. Told against the background of the church's acceptance of slavery the story arrests the hearer. We find a similar message in the first reading. The person who hates his brother or sister walks about with the lie's head upon his shoulders—even though he has been baptized into the truth.

Intercessions

For the gift of discernment to recognize falsehood;
For all women through whose hearts a sword has been plunged.

Prayer

God of Sacred Truth,
  teach us the enormity of every form of deceit,
whether in the private or the public domain,
  with friend or foe.
Let us be true disciples of your Son,
  who is the Way, the Truth, and the Life. Amen.

204   December 30
Sixth Day in the Octave of Christmas

1 John 2:12-17; Luke 2:36-40

Let not the widows be wanderers about, nor fond of dainties, nor gadders from house to house; but let them be like Judith, noted for her seriousness; and like Anna eminent for her sobriety.
                    (Ignatius of Antioch, *To the Smyrneans* 13)

La Maestra era pura. "Los suaves hortelanos,"
decía, "de este predio que es predio de Jesús,
han de conservar puros los ojos y las manos,
guardar claros sus óleos, para dar clara luz."

La Maestra era pobre, Su reino no es humano.
(Así en el doloroso sembrador de Israel.)
Vestía sayas pardas, no enjoyaba su mano.
Y era todo su espíritu un inmenso joyel!
                    (Gabriela Mistral, "La Maestra Rural," *Antologia*)

Prominent in today's reading is the widow, Anna. In our day men and women scholars have pursued considerable research on the subject of widows in the early church. These women were, perhaps, the freest of all women for they were neither under the authority of a father or a husband. Older widows were formally enrolled in the church and given a number of ministries including teaching women. Among the advantages enjoyed by widows were:

freedom from patriarchy;
management of their own wealth;
mobility;
freedom from childbearing and child care (if their children were
  adults)

the ability to offer hospitality to missionaries and other Christians;
perhaps more opportunity for education;
use of their own time and
respect within the community.

Ignatius told the recipients of his letters to honour the widow as if she were the "altar." Thus Luke's account of Anna may indeed reflect practices of the early Christian widows who were seen as wise women who made a great contribution to the church. In fact, they were honored even more than virgins. Job says "I caused the widow's heart to sing for joy" (Job 29:13).

Intercessions

That widows may again grace the church with active ministry;

That all war widows may receive comfort and material help.

Prayer

Counsellor of the Bereaved,
Compassionate Defender of the Widow and the Orphan,
call now these women to active service.
Endow them with your wisdom,
make them fountains of your joy and care. Amen.

205 December 31
Seventh Day in the Octave of Christmas

1 John 2:18-21; John 1:1-18

My idea of God is not a divine idea. It has to be shattered time after time. He shatters it Himself. He is the great iconoclast.
(C. S. Lewis, *A Grief Observed*)

. . .

La belleza y el bien que no miden;
el carbón superado en los diamantes;
el fuego alado y el alado aire,
todo está en Ti, todo eres Tú, Tú eres,
¡Oh. Padre Universal, extenso Padre!
(Juana de Ibarbourou, "Dios," *Once Grandes*, 275)

The Son came to interpret God, who is our father and our mother.

Our image or concept of God is vitally important. It dictates our comportment, it directs our prayer and influences deeply our association with others. A God of judgment will inspire us to penitential and ascetic practices; a God of love to compassion and concern for others. Above all our image of God affects our theology. The portrayals of God in the Hebrew Bible are rich and various, from the God of war and victory to God as mother and midwife. But when Jesus came our image of God was utterly transformed. Now we see God born through the labor pains of a woman, we see a hungry God, a God dealing with the problems of adolescence, a God who goes "to calamities' depth" on the cross for his people. S/he embraces the suffering and degradation of people who are on the lowest rung of the social ladder. Sallie McFague has written an important book named *Models of God*.[4] As well as the traditional images of God she sees God as mother, lover and friend. She says:

> The particular models of mother, lover, and friend, which come from the deepest level of life and are concerned with its fulfillment, have been suggested as illuminating possibilities for expressing an inclusive, nonhierarchical understanding of the gospel. It has been claimed that the object of this gospel is not individuals but the world, and it has been proposed that the world—the cosmos or universe—be seen as God's body. (87)

Intercessions

> That God may become to us mother-father, lover, and friend;
>
> That the church may be in reality a discipleship of equals.

Prayer

> O Most Beloved and Most Profound,
>   your essence defies our human expression.
> Let us draw near to you in silence and in symbol,
>   in cosmic contemplation and
>   in the reflection of your majesty
>   in every human face and gesture. Amen.

[4]Philadelphia: Fortress Press, 1973.

18 January 1
The Solemnity of Mary

Num 6:22-27; Gal 4:4-7; Luke 2:16-21

All of you who have been baptized into Christ have clothed your-
selves with him. There does not exist among you Jew or Greek,
slave or freeman, male or female. All are one in Christ Jesus.
(Gal 3:27-28)

Cristo moreno
pasa
de lirio de Judea
a clavel de España.

¡Miradlo por dónde viene!
(Federico García Lorca, "Poema de la Saeta," *Selected Poems*, 22)

This feast used to be known as the Circumcision of Jesus. Compara-
tively recently it was altered to the Solemnity of Mary. The change
is interesting. According to Genesis 17 God commanded Abraham to
circumcise his sons and his male servants. Jesus, as a Jewish boy, was
obliged to be circumcised. He had to bear the physical sign of the covenant of the chosen people with God. But there is no history of female
circumcision in Judaism. Therefore, women converts to Judaism un-
derwent a ritual bath and recited a confession of their faith. There was
no public ceremony to initiate Jewish girls into the community and only
certain laws were incumbent on them. They were separated from the
men in the Temple and occupied a less prestigious place in society in
general.

All this was changed with Christianity. The initiation rite for Christians was baptism which brought the Spirit and admitted all, irrespec-
tive of race, gender or status, into the covenant between God and the
people. After considerable discussion, the early Church decided not
to require male circumcision of adult nonJewish men who accepted
Christianity. Baptism became the mutual, inclusive rite which initiated
all persons into their relationship with the risen Christ.

Thus this feast could be very meaningful to all Christians, especially
to women. We celebrate the Solemnity of Mary because by God's
choice she became the most important human figure in salvation history. Perhaps one could even say that she was more important than
people like Moses, Elijah, and John the Baptist. In Mary we see the
perfect disciple of Jesus. When Luke describes Pentecost he places Mary
in the center of the worshipping Christian community in the Upper

Room in Jerusalem. She is the only person mentioned by name except the eleven apostles. Thus in Mary we celebrate a discipleship of equals within the Church. The Holy Spirit comes upon Mary in the Annunciation (Luke 1:26-38) and upon the whole community together with Mary on the Feast of Pentecost (Acts 2:1-13).

Intercessions

For friendship with Mary;

For equality between men and women.

Prayer

Covenant God, you called Mary as your true disciple
and the mother of your Son.
Call the Church to recognize in women
disciples filled with the Spirit
to whom the calling of Mary has been bequeathed. Amen.

206 January 2

1 John 2:22-28; John 1:19-28

A prophet comforts the afflicted
and afflicts the comfortable.

Despierto está sobre nosotros, como una
estrella protectora en nuestro cielo.
En el hogar que nos reúne, su nombre augusto
es como el pan y como el fuego.
No hay argentino que no sienta dentro
del alma la virtud de su recuerdo.
(Franciso Luis Bernárdez, "El Libertador," *Los Derechos*, 322)

The gospel reading impresses us with the stark truth of John the Baptist's confession. His questioners wanted to give him a title, a role. He answered that he was an incorporal voice. His rugged simplicity, his blunt, unequivocal message, his readiness to "decrease" so that the Coming One might "increase" and his assertion that he was not fit to do the lowliest of all duties for Jesus fill us with awe—especially as we know that some people wished to make him Messiah. It is no wonder that Jesus declared that he was the greatest of those born of woman. John teaches all pioneers that the time always comes when they must step back so that others may take their place. Unlike the Antichrist in the first reading John denies himself and confesses Christ. It is a fearless and self-effacing confession.

Intercessions

For the humility and courage which characterized John;

For an appreciation of the anointing of baptism and the ability to place our gifts at the service of others.

Prayer

God of Mission and Retirement,
teach us the secrets
of selfless service.
May we discern when to minister
and when to wait, give us patience
that the planted seed may grow. Amen.

207   January 3

1 John 2:29–3:6; John 1:29-34

The tragedy of love is indifference.
(W. Somerset Maugham, *The Trembling of a Leaf*, ch. 4)

There is nothing harder than the softness of indifference.
(Juan Montalvo, *Chapters Forgotten by Cervantes*, Epilogue)

The death of democracy is not likely to be an assassination from ambush. It will be a slow extinction from apathy, indifference and undernourishment.   (R. Maynard Hutchins, *Great Books*)

¡La vida! . . . Polvo en el viento volador.
(Ramón del Valle-Inclán, *El Pasajero, Antologia*, 343)

We could say that the principal motif in our readings today is "privilege." The reading from 1 John speaks in ecstatic terms of our privilege in being God's own children on this earth and of the further blessing of being like Christ in the world to come. In the Gospel John exuberantly identifies Jesus as the Chosen One and as the Lamb of

God who takes away the sin of the world. God granted to John the privilege of unique revelation, the ability to identify the Savior.

Sometimes we take everything for granted: our election by God, our baptism, our membership of the Christian community, our literacy, and a host of other privileges. But above all we are often apathetic with respect to the privilege of knowing Christ as Friend. The opposite of Love is not Hate but Indifference. G. B. Shaw's words are appropriate:

> *The worst sin towards our fellow creatures is not to hate them,*
> *but to be indifferent to them: that's the essence of inhumanity.*
> (*The Devil's Disciple*, Act II)

Intercessions

For excitement over our status as children of God;

For the eradication of all social sin.

Prayer

O God, passionate and hot in your love for your people,
  you threaten to spew
from your mouth the lukewarm.[5]
  Forgive the pittance of our affection.
Ignite us with the Spirit's zeal,
  with the fire of your own ardor. Amen.

208 January 4

1 John 3:7-10; John 1:35-42

Let a new earth rise. Let another world be born. . . . Let a beauty full of healing and a strength of final clenching be the pulsing of our spirits and our blood.
(Margaret Abigail Walker, *For My People*)

Cuerpo de la mujer, río de oro
donde, hurdidos los brazos, recibimos
un relámpago azul, unos racimos
de luz rasgada en un frondor de oro.
(Blas de Otero, "Cuerpo de la Mujer," *Recent Poetry*, 86)

[5]Revelation 3:16.

Our image of Jesus as Lamb of God is patient of many interpretations. Sometimes it conjures up a picture of a woolly lamb in a shepherd's arms; sometimes a lamb sacrificed on the altar; sometimes the lamb whose blood was smeared on the door posts and lintel of the homes of the Israelites and secured them against the death of the first born or at other times we imagine the lamb as the bellwether of the flock, the rampant ram. Not many of these images associate the lamb or his blood with Mary. Yet when we speak of our redemption through "the blood of the Lamb," we are speaking about redemption through the blood originating from a woman's body, Mary's menstrual blood which nurtured Jesus for nine months in her uterus. Mary is the source of the blood of the Lamb of God. And this blood is not shed blood but blood as the source of life. It is the blood which engendered the child begotten of God, the Holy Spirit, within a woman's body. It is the blood which flowed through Jesus' veins and energized the living Savior who healed, taught, loved and eventually allowed this blood to flow from his body on the cross as an act of friendship for humankind: for there is no greater love than to lay down one's life for another. The Lamb's blood, therefore, is life-giving blood. It is woman's blood.

Intercessions

That we may recognize Mary's role in salvation history;

That woman's blood may be seen as holy.

Prayer

God of Infinite Creativity and Profound Delicacy,
*   you chose a woman's body and blood*
for the conception and birth of your Son.
*   That body and blood*
has been broken, poured out, abused
*   throughout the ages.*
Reveal to men and women of our own time
*   the ways of healing and resurrection. Amen.*

209 January 5

1 John 3:11-21; John 1:43-51

A wholesome tongue is a tree of life. . . . (Prov 15:4)

"Yo soy la luz." Miraba hacia la tarde.
Un polvo gris caía tenue, lento.
Era la vida un soplo, un dulce engaño;
sombra, suspiro, sueño.

. . .
"Yo soy la luz." Silencio. "Soy . . . Oídme . . ."
Espacio. Olivo. Cielo.
"Yo soy la luz." Su voz era un susurro.
El aire, ceniciento.
    (Carlos Bousoño, "Cristo en la Tarde," *Los Derechos*, 65)

The first lesson reminds us that Christian witness is nothing without love. In the Gospel lesson, even in the light of Nathanael's perhaps scathing remark—"Can anything good come out of Nazareth?"—Jesus addresses him with love and warmth. He discerns in him a man innocent of deceit. Jesus' compliment illicits from Nathanael the confession of Jesus' status as Son of God and King of Israel. On his side Jesus accepts his tribute and reveals to him that he will see even greater things. Jesus is thinking of Jacob's dream in which he saw angels ascending and descending a heavenly ladder and Jacob's declaration that he was in the presence of God, "the abode of God," the "gateway to heaven." Today's ostensibly simple dialogue contains deep theological truths and may well have been an example of either Jesus' conversation with his disciples or, more likely, the theological reflection of the post Easter Christian community.

Intercessions

For the ability to converse naturally and simply with God;
For a deepening of faith in theologians.

Prayer

O God of Compassion,
  you talked to Moses
    face to face,
      as to a friend.
        Grant us this same grace. Amen.

210 January 6

1 John 5:5-13; Mark 1:7-11

And these are the ways of these (Spirits) in the world.
It is of the Spirit of truth to enlighten the heart of man,
and to level before him the ways of true righteousness,
and to set fear in his heart of the judgment of God.
And (to it belong) the spirit of humility and forbearance,
of abundant mercy and eternal goodness,
of understanding and intelligence,
and almighty wisdom with faith in all the works of God
and trust in His abundant grace. . . .
    (Rule of the Community, Qumran 4:2-6, trans. Dupont-Somer)

Los Reyes Inmortales, tres tenues visionarios
en ronda blanca contra la eternidad azur,
pasarán esta noche, sobre sus dromedarios,
de Oriente hacia Occidente y de Norte hacia Sur.
Y en ciudades enormes y en pueblos solitarios,
en todos los lugares de sus itinerarios,
las cornucopias de oro verterán al albur.
    (Ezequiel Martínez Estrada, ''Bienvenida a Los Reyes
Magos,'' *Antologia*, 886)

John's reference to the threefold witness of the water, the blood and Spirit is enigmatic. It is, however, probably related to the threefold symbolism of baptism. There is baptism with water, exemplified by the baptism of John the Baptist and of many people in the ancient world. It symbolized the remission of sin and, sometimes, initiation into a new community. However, there is also the baptism of suffering (Luke 12:50), a total immersion in physical, psychological and spiritual anguish. There is also the baptism of the Spirit as seen, for example, in Acts 2; 8; 10–11 and 17, when there is an experience of the presence of God and of the Spirit's gifts and fruits. In his Gospel John has brought all these together in the final scene on the cross. Jesus bows his head and gives up his spirit. But here is one of John's typical double meanings, for the Greek phrase can mean ''handed on the Spirit.'' Then the soldiers pierce Jesus' side and there gushes out water and blood. So the cross itself symbolizes a threefold type of baptism.

Intercessions

For a true baptism of the Spirit;
For the gifts of the life-giving Spirit.

Prayer

God, Author and Implementer of Our Salvation,
*   you have mysteriously baptized us into your Son,*
immersed us in his resurrected presence.

Help us not to shun the baptism of suffering
or to be indifferent to the gifts of the Spirit. Amen.

19 Second Sunday after Christmas
Cycles A, B, and C

Sir 24:1-4, 8-12; Eph 1:3-6, 15-18; John 1:1-18

For she (Wisdom) is an aura of the might of God
and a pure effusion of the glory of the Almighty. . . .

For she is the refulgence of eternal light,
the spotless mirror of the power of God,
the image of his goodness.   (Wis 7:25-26)

Siempre la claridad viene del cielo;
es un don: no se halla entre las cosas
sino muy por encima, y las ocupa
haciendo de ello vida y labor propias.
Así amanece el día; así la noche
cierra el gran aposento de sus sombras.
Y esto es un don.

(Claudio Rodríguez, "Siempre La Claridad Viene
Del Cielo," *Anthology of Spanish Poetry*, 164)

The overriding theme of our readings is wisdom. In the Jewish Scriptures there is an interesting and emotive development in the theology of wisdom. In Proverbs 8–9 she is presented as a woman teacher calling disciples to her feast of wisdom symbolized by meat, bread and wine. In our first reading we are told that she existed at the beginning of creation and assisted in that creation. She was called by God to be God's immanence in the world and chose Jerusalem as her abode. Further, throughout the whole of the *Wisdom of Solomon* she is portrayed as a redeemer figure, and in chapter seven she is given clear divine attributes (see the quotation above). She becomes, in effect, the female aspect of the deity. She is not a separate being but the epitome of feminine grace in God. Later in Jewish thought she is known as the Shekinah, the Royal Presence. The prologue of John's Gospel (our third reading) is obviously influenced by the theology of wisdom. Jesus is seen as the Incarnate Wisdom, coming down to his chosen people to dwell among them.

Intercessions

For God's blessing on professional women;

For a harmony among all members of the church.

Prayer

God, you are our Father and our Mother,
in you we find the plenitude of
all femininity and masculinity.
Grant us wisdom, the refulgence of eternal light,
so that men and women, as equal partners,
may realize all their potential. Amen.

20 January 6
or the Sunday occurring from January 2 to 8 inclusive
The Epiphany

Isa 60:1-6; Eph 3:2-3, 5-6; Matt 2:1-12

We hold these truths to be self-evident,
that all men and women are created equal.
> (E. C. Stanton, *First Women's Rights Convention*)

Virtue can only flourish amongst equals.
> (Mary Wollstonecraft, *A Vindication of the Rights of Men*)

Los Reyes Inmortales, tres tenues visionarios
en ronda blanca contra la eternidad azur,
pasáran esta noche, sobre sus dromedarios,
de Oriente hacia Occidente y de Norte hacia Sur.
Y en ciudades enormes y en pueblos solitarios,
en todos los lugares de sus itinerarios,
las cornucopias de oro vertarán al albur.
> (Ezequiel Martínezs Estrada, "Bienvenida a los Reyes Magos," *Antologia*, 886)

The last two Sundays have led us to consider the place of woman and femininity in salvation history. Today's reading leads us to reflect upon non-Jewish peoples, that is, the Gentiles, who are also brought to the fullness of grace in the Christian dispensation so that they become, as Paul says, "co-heirs with the Jews . . . sharers of the promise through the preaching of the gospel." The struggle to include Gentiles on an equal basis with Jewish Christians was not easy. The Jewish people practiced marital laws, dietary regulations, sexual *mores*, purificationary laws, observance of the sabbath and male circumcision which many Gentiles found difficult to accept. There were even restrictions with regard to with whom one could dine and this was a serious difficulty with respect to the celebration of the Eucharist. However, through the inspiration of the Spirit and the work, especially of Peter (Acts 10:1–11:18) and Paul, the Gentiles were admitted into the church with all the rights and privileges of the Jewish Christians. If this had not happened most of us would not be in the Church today. The wise men and women whom Matthew represents as coming to worship Jesus were probably Gentiles. They offered gold, frankincense and myrrh or as the gypsy in one of Robertson Davies' novels says, "Gold, frank innocence and mirth!" (*Lyre of Orpheus*). Thus Epiphany is the feast *par excellence* for the universality of the Church.

Intercessions

> For astronomers and all scientists that they may bring, not death,
>   but life to our world;
> For a just distribution of the wealth of nations.

Prayer

> God of All Peoples,
>   you called Christianity to be a world religion.
> Forgive our past animosity against Jews and Moslems,
>   and bring us to a closer understanding,
>   through Jesus Christ who is the Prince of Peace. Amen.

211 January 7

1 John 5:14-21; John 2:1-12

The miracles in fact are a retelling in small letters of the very same story which is written across the whole world in letters too large for some of us to see.

(C. S. Lewis, *God in the Dock*)

Nada te turbe;
nada te espante;
todo se pasa;
Dios no se muda,
la paciencia
todo lo alcanza,
quien a Dios tiene,
nada le falta.
Sólo Dios basta.

(St. Teresa's bookmark, *Anthology of Spanish Poetry*, 71)

John's miracles, which he calls "signs," are carefully selected and all contain a deep theological mystery. They are signs which point beyond themselves. Thus in this Cana miracle we first see Jesus as an ordinary wedding guest with his family and friends. But the wedding became a means of theological revelation when, at the bidding of his mother, he turned the water into delicious wine. The wedding is the symbol of the covenant relationship of God and the chosen people, especially that established on Mount Sinai. God is bridegroom and the people are the bride. This metaphor is much elaborated in Jewish writings dated later than the New Testament. When Jesus plays this crucial part in the wedding feast, he indicates the dawn of the messianic age when, symbolically, water will be changed to wine, that is, there will be a new creation. One mark of John's Gospel is that the Jewish feasts are brought to their fullest expression by Jesus; for example, Hanukkah—the Feast of Lights, Tabernacles, Passover and, possibly, the Day of Atonement. So those feasts which re-enacted key points in salvation history are reinterpreted by Jesus and brought to perfection. Immediately after the Cana episode John reports that Jesus cleansed the Temple in Jerusalem. The other Gospels place the incident in the passion era of Jesus' ministry but John wishes to emphasize that Jesus renewed the whole spiritual life of Israel.

Intercessions

For the avoidance of all deadly sin;
For an acceptance of the new revelation given in Jesus.

Prayer

God of Conviviality,
  at the request of a woman
you turned water into wine.
  Grant us the gift to grace
    all mundane matters
  with the transforming charm
    of your joyous Spirit. Amen.

213 January 7 or Monday after Epiphany

1 John 3:22-4:6; Matt 4:12-17, 23-25

May you be blessed in your coming in,
and blessed in your going out!   (Deut 28:6)

¡Oh noche que guiaste!
¡Oh noche amable más que el alborada!
¡Oh noche que juntaste
Amado con amada,
Amada en el amado transformada!

> (Juan de la Cruz, "La Noche Oscura,"
> *Anthology of Spanish Poetry,* 77)

Our reading puts before us the doctrine of the two ways, the way of evil and the way of good. We find this theme in the book of Deuteronomy where Moses places before the people the option of blessing and life or cursing and death. It appears again in the Dead Sea Scroll documents where it is expressed in the terms of the Spirit of Truth and the Spirit of Perversity, or the People of the Light and the People of Darkness. It is used also in the New Testament and continued in early Christian writings, for example, the *Shepherd of Hermas.* The two ways emphasize human freewill. It is the responsibility of man and woman to make a choice between these ways. For this we need discernment and courage. The choice of life is the way through the narrow door (Matt 7:14) but it is a way strewn with blessings. As the Dead Sea Scrolls depict it:

> *As for the Visitation of all who walk in this (Spirit, i.e. the Spirit*
> *of Truth),*
> *it consists in healing and abundance of bliss,*
> *with length of days and fruitfulness,*
> *and all blessings without end,*
> *and eternal joy in perpetual life,*
> *and the glorious crown and garment of honour in everlasting life.*
> > *(The Rule of the Community,* Qumran 3:8,
> > trans. Dupont-Somer)

These are the gifts which we receive if we walk in the Spirit of Truth. In the Gospels we see Jesus bringing the Spirit of Light to all who are in the darkness of oppression, hunger and degradation. He himself is filled with the Spirit of Truth.

Intercessions

That we may choose the path of Light;

That Christ, the Sun of Healing, may cherish those racked with pain.

Prayer

Parent of Solar Light,
  you, yourself, cannot change or be overshadowed.
We mourn because, in our human frailty,
  darkness, confusion, discord and rigor
have often come in the wake of religion.
  Teach us that ''pure religion and undefiled''
is to care for the underprivileged
  and to bring unity and love to humankind. Amen.

214 January 8 or Tuesday after Epiphany

1 John 4:7-10; Mark 6:34-44

No coward soul is mine,
No trembler in the world's storm-troubled sphere;
I see Heaven's glories shine,
And faith shines equal, arming me from fear.

(Emily Brontë, *Last Lines*)

True nobility is exempt from fear.

(Shakespeare, *Henry VI*, 4.1.129)

Madre antigua y atroz de la incestuosa guerra,
Borrado sea tu nombre de la faz de la tierra.

(Jorge Luis Borges, "El Hombre," *Los Derechos*, 456)

The first reading states that if we love one another, God abides in us and love is perfected. Those who love are of one Spirit and because it is the nature of love to grow and increase the more it is divided the only way to perfect love is to share. This is graphically symbolized in the multiplication of loaves. The result of our love is the bestowal of the Spirit. We become almost "another self" of God, just as a friend is "another self." Faith in Jesus also causes the Spirit to dwell in us. This love and faith are the unique features of covenant love which in Hebrew is called ḥesed. Ḥesed is difficult to translate; it is all that is good, harmonious, health-bringing, faithful and cherishing in the relationship between covenant partners. In the gospel reading, we see this compassionate love and effective faith in the person of Jesus, who multiplies the bread and fish so that there might be a unique community sharing, an equality of distribution and a discipleship of equals. The "leftovers" show that sharing of goods is always more than sufficient. It is abundance.

Intercessions

That we may be able to discern the image and likeness of God in the needy;

That we might gain some understanding of being "begotten" by God.

Prayer

Doctor of All Ills,
   come with your healing mercy
      to those bruised by human conflict,
         to those confused by bereavement,
            to those destitute by flood, fire or earthquake.
   Remember us when we are broken
      by trivialities. Amen.

215   January 9 or Wednesday after Epiphany

1 John 4:11-18; Mark 6:45-52

We must surely believe that the divine charity is as fertile in re-
source as it is measureless in condescension.
                              (C. S. Lewis, *The World's Last Night*)

Tu presencia encima de todo, lo que hablo,
debajo de una roca donde no estoy,
tú en el triunfo extraño que es amor. . . .
                  (Pureza Canelo, "La Luz," *Recent Poetry*, 324)

   In the first reading, John once again dwells on love. Just as two married persons become one flesh, so those who love God become one
Spirit with him. This love casts out fear for, to some extent, fear is lack
of confidence or the lack of knowledge of the other, a certain insecurity. One of the greatest compliments that one can pay to another is
to be able to speak frankly, even to confront him or her, without fear
of anger or reprisal. Perfect love casts out fear. There will be no fear
in heaven, in eternal life, and the Johannine Jesus teaches that those
who love and believe him even now have eternal life. So fearless love
is an anticipation of eternity where there will be perfect communication and understanding. This victory over fear is seen in the Gospel
for Jesus conquers the fear of the disciples by proclaiming his presence and calming the storm of the sea and the "storm" within their
hearts.

Intercessions

For those who live in constant fear;
For an overwhelming sense of the presence of Christ.

Prayer

O Infinite Patience, Boundless Understanding,
  enter our fragile hearts,
    storm-tossed by the darkness of fear and mistrust.
Cast your warm light around us
  to melt every shadow of insecurity. Amen.

216   January 10 or Thursday after Epiphany

1 John 4:19-5:4; Luke 4:14-22

Religion cannot be kept within the bounds of sermons and scrip-
tures. It is a force in itself and it calls for the integration of lands
and peoples in harmonious unity. The lands [of the planet] wait
for those who can discern their rhythms. The peculiar genius of
each continent, each river valley, the rugged mountains, the placid
lakes, all call for relief from the constant burden of exploitation.
(Vine Victor Deloria, Jr. [A Standing Rock
Sioux], God is Red)

Ojos indígenas, absortos,
que están como soñando,
que están como perdidos
en la desolación del altiplano.

Ojos aymaras que no han visto
nada más que los campos
ilímites, sin nadie,
fatigadoramente rasos.
(Gregorio Reynolds, "Ojos," Los Derechos, 198–199)

The reading from John equates lack of love for a brother or sister with lack of love for God. This can be seen in two ways. Firstly, through our adoption into God's family all are our brothers and sisters; and secondly, to hate a brother is to hate God's own image and likeness in whom we were made. In the gospel reading, Jesus' prophetic proclamation of the Jubilee means, in essence, a love of neighbors and brothers and sisters. In the Jubilee year according to Leviticus 25:8-55: debts were forgiven; slaves were released; land was returned to its original owner; the land was given her "sabbath" and, perhaps, prisoners were released. In other words there was redistribution of land

and wealth and a restoration of human dignity for each person. Luke makes this proclamation of the Jubilee the inaugural scene of Jesus' ministry. In doing so he stresses that it is a ministry directly associated with social justice and love. Jesus, the Begotten of God, conquers the world's injustice.

Intercessions

That we richer nations may effect a Jubilee year for third world countries;

That a prophetic witness may emerge within the Church and society.

Prayer

Covenant God,
  you did allot the land of Israel equably
according to the number of persons in each tribe.
  Grant to our greedy and ambitious world
the wisdom and charity
  to seek for a just distribution of land.
Let us respect the sacred nature
  of territorial boundaries. Amen.

217 January 11 or Friday after Epiphany

1 John 5:5-13; Luke 5:12-16

Joy is Love's consciousness;
Peace is Love's confidence;
Long-temperness (patience) is Love's habit;
Kindness is Love's activity;
Goodness is Love's quality;
Faithfulness is Love's quantity;
Meekness is Love's tone;
Temperance is Love's victory.   (Campbell Morgan)

. . .

Dios no es rey ni parece rey,
Dios no es suntuoso ni rico.
Dios lleva en sí la humana grey
Y todo su inmenso acerico.

. . .

Dios está de nueva manera,
Y viene a familia de obrero,
Sindicato de la madera.
El humilde es el verdadero. . . .

(Jorge Guillén, "Epifanía," *Penguin Book of Spanish Verse*, 437)

The first reading raises the question, "What does it mean to possess eternal life?" John speaks about our possessing eternal life even now. It comprises the possession of the fruits of the Spirit—love, joy, peace, patience, kindness, generosity, faithfulness, gentleness, self control. These are eternal because they are the essential attributes of God and can never fail. When Christians possess them they begin to enjoy eternal life. The gospel lesson complements this by speaking of the cure of the leper. This was much more than a physical cure. It was also a familial, social and religious healing because the patient could return to family life, play an active part in social life and once again join his religious community and worship in the synagogue and even the Temple. In a similar way the fruits of the Spirit lead us as individuals and as a society.

Intercessions

For the fruits of the Spirit;
For wholeness of life.

Prayer

God, you have deftly wrought
the union of godhood and humanhood
in the incarnation of Jesus.
Grant that we, your begotten children,
may live worthy of our high calling
and savor the fruits of the Spirit
even upon this earth. Amen.

218 January 12 or Saturday after Epiphany

1 John 5:14-21; John 3:22-30

It is not chastening but liberating to know that one has always been almost wholly superfluous; wherever one has done well some other has done all the real work . . .

(C. S. Lewis, "Taliessin Through Logres," 4, 8)

. . .

Quedéme y olvidéme,
el rostro reclíné sobre el Amado,
cesó todo, y dejéme,
dejando mi cuidado
entre las azucenas olvidado.

(San Juan de la Cruz, "Canción de la subida del Monte Carmelo," *Penguin Book of Spanish Poetry*, 221)

The gospel lesson gives us a glimpse of the humble greatness of the Baptist. He holds no grudge because Jesus is more popular than he; he recognizes God working in Jesus and his own role as human and he is ready to decrease that Jesus might increase. A very powerful figure of speech is used here. John employs the metaphor of marriage which figure is so much loved in the Hebrew Scriptures, God as bridegroom taking to himself the bride, Israel. John sees himself as the friend of the bridegroom, Jesus, the Son and Agent of God. As friend of the groom John must meticulously oversee all the varied and multifarious preparations for the wedding. The friend's last duty was to stand outside the door of the chamber or tent in which the groom and the bride consummated their marriage. The groom on his wedding day was exempt from reciting the *Shema*, the prayer which begins "Hear, O Israel, the Lord thy God is One Lord. . . ." This was said at sunrise and sunset. However, after the successful consummation of the marriage the groom recited the *Shema* aloud and when the friend of the groom heard this he rejoiced and went on his way. His task was happily and successfully fulfilled. In John's case God's commitment to the divine covenant had reached its climax in the incarnation, the union of godhood and humanhood. John hears Jesus' joyful cry of consummation and goes on his way.

Intercessions

For the deference of John the Baptist;
For joy over the success of others.

Prayer

Meticulous Planner of Salvation,
you have woven together
the human and the divine.
Grant us never to sunder this sacred union. Amen.

21 Sunday after January 6th
The Baptism of the Lord

Isa 42:1-4, 6-7; Acts 10:34-38; Matt 3:13-17

Know you what it is to be a child? It is to be something very differ-
ent from the man of today. It is to have a spirit yet streaming from
the waters of baptism; it is to believe in love, to believe in loveli-
ness, to believe in belief; it is to be so little that the elves can reach
to whisper in your ear . . . for each child has its fairy godmother
in its soul.　　　　　　　　(Shelley, *Dublin Review*, July 1908)

Deep, unspeakable suffering may well be called a baptism, a regener-
ation, the initiation into a new state.　　(George Eliot, *Adam Bede*)

Inclina
más mi frente—esta frente siempre alta . . .
Suaviza
Y distiende mis manos que, de tanto
no querer asir nada, están un poco rígidas. . . .
Inclíname la frente alta y devuélvele
a tu tierra mi mirada perdida.
¡Ay! miré demasiado las estrellas. . . .
No hay que mirarlas tanto. . . .
　　　　　　(Dulce Maria Loynaz, "La Oracion del Alba,"
　　　　　　　　　　　　　　　　　　　Once Grandes, 399)

We often think of baptism merely as a purification from sin but this
leads to a problem. Why was Jesus, who was innocent, baptized?
Through his experience we can see that baptism is the answer to a call
from God, the realization of election by God. Genuine response to this
call allows us to be born into a new way of life and this birth takes
place in the midst of the community. It gives the candidate responsibility towards and support from that community.

Thus our first reading addresses the discipleship of the Servant of the Lord whom Christians recognized in Jesus. The Servant is gentle and brings light and healing to the nations, both Jew and Gentile. The second reading shows Peter baptizing the first Gentiles into the community. The gospel lesson for each lectionary cycle shows God's confirmation of Jesus' mission to the people. It is a mission greater than that of John the Baptist and it is one in which all his brothers and sisters share. Baptism gives every person, man, woman and child, the offices of priest, prophet and king (queen) and calls them to exercise these ministries.

We might reflect on the words of Thomas Cranmer at the baptism of Queen Elizabeth (as portrayed by Shakespeare):

This royal infant, (Heaven still move about her!)
Though in her cradle, yet now promises
Upon this land a thousand thousand blessings,
Which time shall bring to ripeness.
. . . truth shall nurse her,
Holy and heavenly thoughts still counsel her:
She shall be loved, and dear'd: her own shall bless her. . . .
                                                        (*Henry VIII*, 5.4.17–30)

Intercessions

For godparents, that they may accept their responsibility with wisdom and sincerity;

For peaceful relationships between Jews, Muslims and Christians.

Prayer

God of Promise and Fulfillment,
   you have elected all your people
to be your special possession.
   Grant us to covet wisdom,
to be jealous for integrity.
   Through your graceful presence among us
may all the habitants of the earth
   reap the harvest
of goodness and justice. Amen.

305 Monday of the First Week of the Year

Heb 1:1-6; 1 Sam 1:1-8; Mark 1:14-20

True happiness
Consists not in the multitude of friends,
But in the worth and choice.   (Ben Jonson, *Cynthia's Revels*)

Así pudieras ser águila
sobre los hombres; abiertos
los ojos, mirando al sol
cara a cara.
(Gloria Fuertes, "Amigo Mirando al Sol," *Antología*, Cano, 249)

Our main theme for all three readings is God's planned, free and loving election. In the reading from Hebrews, Jesus comes as Son of God as the crown of all the prophetic aspirations; in the second text Elkanah shows his constant love for Hannah, his chosen wife, even though she was despised in her society because she had not born a son. In the gospel reading, Jesus calls his first disciples and they respond immediately and without reserve.

God's choice means friendship with the divine and friendship among men and women. In his exposition of friendship (*De Amicitia*) Cicero, the famous Roman orator, says:

> *For friendship is nothing else than an accord in all things, human and divine, conjoined with mutual goodwill and affection, and I am inclined to think that, with the exception of wisdom, no better thing has been given to man by the immortal gods . . . friendship offers advantages almost beyond my power to describe. . . .*
> *What is sweeter than to have someone with whom you may dare discuss anything as if you were communing with yourself? How could your enjoyment in times of prosperity be so great if you did not have someone whose joy in them would be equal to your own?*
> *. . . he who looks upon a true friend, looks, as it were, upon a sort of image of himself.*   (Cicero, *De Amicitia*)

Intercessions

For childless men and women;
For a true understanding of friendship.

Prayer

God, you have taught us that wisdom
makes friends and prophets.
Help us to choose our friends wisely
and commit ourselves faithfully.
Lead us to that unique friendship
which comes only through your beloved Son. Amen.

306 Tuesday of the First Week of the Year

Heb 2:5-12; 1 Sam 1:9-20; Mark 1:21-28

The Negro was willing to risk martyrdom in order to move and
stir the social conscience of his community and the nation . . .
he would force his oppressor to commit his brutality openly, with
the rest of the world looking on. . . . Nonviolent resistance para-
lyzed and confused the power structures against which it was
directed.   (Martin Luther King, Jr. *Why We Can't Wait*)

Dos niños, ramas de un mismo árbol de miseria
. . .
Dos niños: uno negro, otro blanco.
            (Nicolás Guillén, "Dos Niños," *Los Derechos*, 217)

Our readings present the idea of a child consecrated to God's service, a child, destined to be a great prophet, conceived after a barren
woman pours out her grief before God (1 Sam 1:9-20) and a child of
God deliberately sent into the world to be one with suffering and death-
fearing humanity (Heb 2:5-12). Most cultures have traditions about the
coming of a hero or heroine who, with courage and perseverance,
tackles and overcomes various difficulties and, in some cases, descends
into the underworld to defeat death and restore life. In Christ we have
a unique and historic example of this. Our author emphasizes Christ's
suffering in total solidarity with humankind, whom, through his obe-
dient suffering, he brings to glory. Glory is the full implementation
of all one's potentials. Thus Christ enables all people to reach the height
of human dignity. In the strength of his Christian conviction Martin
Luther King, Jr. followed in the steps of Christ. He said:

The tortuous road which has led from Montgomery to Oslo is a
road over which millions of Negroes are traveling to find a new
sense of dignity. It will, I am convinced, be widened into a su-
perhighway of justice.

(Martin Luther King, Jr.; Speech accepting the
Nobel Peace Prize, December 11, 1964)

Intercessions

For those whose human dignity is not yet recognized;

For an understanding of the psychology of "demon possession."

Prayer

God, you gave up your beloved Son for us.
  Grant that we, who have received a harvest of justice
reaped from others' suffering,
  may not fail in our debt of gratitude
or in our duty to bequeath it to others. Amen.

307 Wednesday of the First Week of the Year

Heb 2:14-18; 1 Sam 3:1-10; Mark 1:29-39

It is not more strange that there should be evil spirits than evil
men—evil unembodied spirits than evil embodied spirits.

(Samuel Johnson, *Boswell's Tour to the Hebrides*)

. . .

como arpa de David da refrigerio
a nuestras almas cuando ya el espíritu
del Malo las tortura . . . .

(Miguel de Unamuno, "El Cristo de Velázquez,"
Antología, Onis, 222)

In our readings today we have an association between the human
being's worst enemy, death, and the devil. To us this may seem to
be a curious connection. But in the ancient world many people were
petrified by demonic activity and saw it as the cause of physical and
mental illness, agricultural failure, shipwrecks, cosmic catastrophes
and, in many incidents, of death itself. Here is a description of one
demon:

Lix Tetrax, who carries his face high in the air, but the rest of his body winding like a snail. He raises a violent dust storm to frighten Solomon. He is busiest in summer, causing colics and fires and semi-tertian fever. . . .   (Testament of Solomon 7)

In the gospel lesson, Jesus cures people possessed by demons. These were probably physical and psychological disturbances found among the socially, economically—and sometimes religiously—deprived persons. Theissen states that demon possession and magic are intensified by social conditions and are especially prevalent among the poorer classes who are without a means of articulating their distress (Gerd Theissen, *Miracle Stories of the Early Christian Tradition*, Philadelphia: Fortress Press, 1983). This may help us to understand the summaries of Jesus' healings and exorcisms which are found in Mark. The miracle stories show the depth of Jesus' compassion, his wish to empathize with people's difficulties, to align himself with the defenseless and the persons who had no human rights and to give them a sense of belonging and hope. The miracle stories promise salvation on a social plane.

However, Jesus not only removes people's fear of these demons but also the fear of death, as an epitaph expresses it: "The long mysterious Exodus of death."[6] Jesus, wholly identifying himself with humanity, begins his long exodus through life, death and resurrection and becomes the guide and companion of all humanity. However, salvation cannot comprise only the healing of all social ills; we would still be left with the hunger for "imperishable bliss." As Stevens says:

She says, "But in contentment I still feel
The need of some imperishable bliss."
Death is the mother of Beauty; hence from her,
Alone, shall come fulfillment of our dreams
And our desires.   (Wallace Stevens, *Sunday Morning*)

The character of our journey through life affects our concept of death. Nin speaks succinctly:

People living deeply have no fear of death.
                (Anaïs Nin, *The Diary of Anïs Nin*)

Jesus assuages the death-pain by his resurrection.

[6]The Jewish Cemetery at Newport, 1858, st. 1.

Intercessions

That people may lose their fear of demons;

That we, like Samuel, might listen attentively to God's call and respond as promptly;

That we, like Jesus, may make time for prayer.

Prayer

God of the Exodus, Liberator of the Poor,
  so accompany us through life
that we may exorcise social ills with cheerful compassion.
  Enable us to fix our gaze on Jesus,
the pioneer and perfecter of our faith. Amen.

308 Thursday of the First Week of the Year

Heb 3:7-14; 1 Sam 4:1-11; Mark 1:40-45

The universal host up sent
A shout that tore hell's concave, and beyond
Frighted the reign of Chaos and old Night.

(Milton, *Paradise Lost*)

And then there crept
A little noiseless noise among the leaves,
Born of the very sigh that silence heaves.

(Keats, *I stood tiptoe upon a Little Hill*)

El Dios que existe es el de los proletarios.

(Ernesto Cardenal, Salmo 57)

Today's readings enable us to focus on the different ways in which God manifests her/his presence. In the reading from Samuel both the Israelites and the Philistines associate fear with the aura of the presence of God surrounding the ark of the covenant. This was a coffin shaped box of acacia wood into which it is said that the Israelites placed the tablets of the ten commandments, a pot of manna and Aaron's rod. It was the empty throne of God which they took into battle. In this text the presence of God is heralded by shouts both on the part of the Israelites and the Philistines. The reading from Hebrews, which is a reflection on Psalm 95, warns us to avoid hardheartedness and to listen attentively to the call of God in our daily lives: it is a call to faith in the midst of difficult circumstances and also a call to a "divine goal" (Harold W. Attridge, *Hebrews*, Hermeneia [Philadelphia: Fortress Press, 1989] 114). In the Jewish Scriptures this divine goal was the promised land of Canaan; for the Christian it is the establishment of God's kingdom. There are different ways of feeling and responding to God's presence.

Intercessions

That we might enter into God's rest even upon this earth;

That we might be delivered from all superstition.

Prayer

God, Author of Sound and Silence,
   teach us to harmonize these your gifts.
In this noisy, restless world,
   allow us to hear your soundless whisper. Amen.

309 Friday of the First Week of the Year

Heb 4:1-5, 11; 1 Sam 8:4-7, 10-22; Mark 2:1-12

He that can take rest is greater than he who can take cities.
                                        (Benjamin Franklin, *Poor Richard's Almanac*)

O rest! thou soft word! autumnal flower of Eden! moonlight of the spirit!   (Jean Paul Richter, *Hesperus*)

El tiempo era sagrado. Los días eran dioses.
                                        (Ernesto Cardenal, *Las ciudadas perdidas*)

The second reading suggests the bustling activity of a powerful and organized kingdom. However, the dominant motif of the first lesson is "rest." It is used in a special theological sense and invites us to enter "that festal sabbath rest that God enjoys" (Attridge, 123–128). Often this was taken to mean eschatological rest, e.g. 4 Ezra 8:52; "for you a paradise is opened . . . a city is built, rest is furnished" (Attridge, 126). Owing to Greek influence the idea of "rest" also came to mean lack of change, "the changeless repose of the divine," the effortless activity of God. Christians seek to share this rest in God's presence. One way of doing this is to celebrate at least one day (not necessarily Sunday) as a day of rest and cultural learning.

Intercessions

That the sabbath may be honored;

That monarchs may not take advantage of their servants.

Prayer

God of Sport and Joy,
  you did marvelously create the human body
and made it holy by the indwelling of wisdom.
  Grant that we may use these gifts
creatively and elegantly
  and find the golden mean
between activity and repose. Amen.

310 Saturday of the First Week of the Year

Heb 4:12-16; 1 Sam 9:1-4, 17-19; 10:1; Mark 2:13-17

Strongest minds are often those of whom the noisy world
Hears least.   (Wordsworth, *The Excursion*)

Virtud es la alegría que alivia el corazón
más grave y desarruga el ceño de Catón.
                    (Antonio Machado, ''Proverbios y Cantares,'' xiii,
                                   Antología, Onis, 282)

All three readings speak of wisdom and insight which penetrate the very heart or essence. Hebrews describes the awesome power of the Word of God, God's own speech. One Jewish writer, Philo, says of the Word of God:

For God, not deeming it meet that sense should perceive Him, sends forth His Words to succor the lovers of virtue, and they act as physicians of the soul and completely heal its infirmities, giving holy exhortations with all the force of irreversible enactments, and call-

ing to the exercise and practice of these and like trainers implant-
ing strength and power and vigor that no adversary can withstand.
                                                      (Philo, *On Dreams*)

1 Samuel shows the perspicacity of Samuel who perceived Saul's ability to be a competent ruler. When Samuel chose his successor, David, as king he said:

Do not judge from his appearance or from his lofty stature. . . .
Not as man sees does God see, because man sees the appearance
but the Lord looks into the heart.   (1 Sam 16:7)

The gospel lesson shows Jesus discerning the hearts of persons whom others regarded as sinners and despicable. In *Michelson's Ghosts*, author John Gardner describes the chief character watching battered men waiting their turn for the service of a prostitute. He observes how the unloved seek for love and the prostitute tries to offer them this. Jesus himself offered a bond of love to the unloved, the tax collector and sinners.

Intercessions

For prostitutes and the unloved;

For those who preach and teach the Word of God.

Prayer

God, Gentle Discerner of the Stumbling Human Heart,
  grant us compassion for the unloved.
Let us learn gratitude from the ungrateful,
  courage from cowards
and love of life
  from the indifferent,
the joyless and the bewildered,
through Jesus our compassionate high priest. Amen.

65   Second Sunday of the Year
Cycle A

Isa 49:3, 5-6; 1 Cor 1:1-3; John 1:29-34

The Providence that's in a watchful state
Knows almost every grain of Plutus' gold;
Finds bottom in th'uncomprehensive deeps;
Keeps place with thought, and almost, like the gods
Doth thoughts unveil in their dumb cradles.

(*Troilus and Cressida*, III, iii, 196–200)

Gracias, Señor, porque estás
todavía en mi palabra;
porque debajo de todos
mis puentes pasan tus aguas.

(Jose Garcia Nieto, "Gracias, Señor," *Antologia* 185)

Our main theme is election, election even before conception. This is closely associated with the all-embracing Wisdom and Providence of God. It is said of the Wisdom of God:

And she, who is one, can do all things,
and renews everything while herself perduring;
And passing into holy souls from age to age,
she produces friends of God and prophets . . .
Indeed, she reaches from end to end mightily
and governs all things well. (Wis 7:27; 8:1)

God's servant in the Isaiah reading has a cosmic mission. In the gospel lesson, John the Baptist sees Jesus himself as predestined by God to take away the sin of the world, that is, to reconcile the world and bring about a friendship between God and humanity. This is only possible through the infusion of the Holy Spirit, Wisdom herself, whom John saw descend upon Jesus.

Intercessions

That we might recognize our own election by God;
That we may invite Lady Wisdom to abide with us.

Prayer

> *God of Wisdom and Intelligent Hope,*
> * you are the meticulous architect of the universe*
> *and the provident pilot of all*
> * through the complexities of life.*
>
> *We bless you for hindsight*
> *which enables us to see your guidance.*
> *We ask you for purity of heart and*
> *singleness of purpose. Amen.*

66   Second Sunday of the Year
Cycle B

1 Sam 3:3-10, 19; 1 Cor 6:13-15, 17-20; John 1:35-42

> *He who throws away a friend is as bad as he who throws away*
> *his life.*   (Sophocles, *Oedipus Rex*)

> *A man cannot speak to his son but as a father, to his wife but as*
> *a husband, to his enemy but upon terms; whereas a friend may*
> *speak as the case requires, and not as it sorteth with the person.*
>   (Francis Bacon, *Essays*)

> *Dios está cerca. El trigo*
> *se dobla como un ángel*
> *anunciador que siente*
> *la bendición del aire . . . .*
>   (Luis Rosales, "Viento en La Carne," *Antologia*, Cano, 80)

We could sum up the main theme of today's readings as "discipleship," the willingness to follow God's call and Jesus' invitation. Discipleship denotes an intimate bond between the Caller and the called. In John 15:15, Jesus calls his followers "friends." It is an interesting fact that the word "disciple" does not occur in Paul's letters. Paul never speaks about his "disciples": for him one can only follow one teacher or master, Jesus, and every minister must try to avoid misusing his/her status and creating their own disciples. As S. Schneider observes in her article on the footwashing, a "deep flaw" may lie in the relationship between server and served, the parent tries to fulfill himself/herself in service to a child; a teacher may make his/her students into trophies, or priests make his parishioners "sheep." Really the only true relation is one of friend to friend ("The Footwashing [John 13:1-20]: An Experiment in Hermeneutics," *Catholic Biblical Quarterly* 43 [1981] 76–92).

Cicero says:

> *For friendship is nothing else than an accord in all things, human and divine, conjoined with mutual goodwill and affection, and I am inclined to think that, with the exception of wisdom, no better thing has been given man(sic) by the immortal gods.*
>
> *(On Friendship)*

This is what discipleship should be.

Intercessions

> *For the awesome power of the listening ear;*
> *For the grace to reverence our bodies as the home of the Holy Spirit.*

Prayer

> *God, Friend of Man, Woman, and Beast,*
>   *draw us with the bonds of love.*
> *May we enter the triune circle of your friendship,*
>   *so that we may be one,*
> *even as you, with the Son and the Spirit are one. Amen.*

67 Second Sunday of the Year
Cycle C

Isa 62:1-5; 1 Cor 12:4-11; John 2:1-12

Our texts speak of weddings. God's covenant is like a marriage bond with his people and Jesus' first sign in John's Gospel was performed at the request of a woman and in an atmosphere of nuptial conviviality. The marriage symbol bespeaks intimacy, love, creativity and joy. As Shakespeare speaks of the union of the lover and beloved:

> *Two lovely berries molded on one stem:*
> *So with two seeming bodies, but one heart.*
>
> *(A Midsummer Night's Dream, 3.2.211–12)*

He also describes close friendship:

> *We still have slept together,*
> *Rose at an instant, learn'd, play'd, eat together;*
> *And wheresoe'er we went, like Juno's swans,*
> *Still we went coupled and inseparable.*
>
> *(As You Like It,* 1.3.69–72)

> *Hombre, casa, mujer,*
> *jóvenes ramas,*
> *se enlazan, se confunden,*
> *forman la triple noche*
> *de la sangre, el cuerpo, del destino.*
>
> (Clara Silva, "Matrimonio," *Once Grandes* 374)

Jesus, in his incarnation, knit together the divine and the human so that they were "coupled" and "inseparable." Thus God appeared in the flesh to grace our joys with the divine presence.

Intercessions

> *For an intimate friendship with God;*
>
> *For a full exercise of the fruits of the Spirit.*

Prayer

> *God of Mirth and Feasting,*
> *enter now into the hearts of all who are depressed.*
> *May your presence expel their gloom*
> *so that your image and likeness*
> *may shine through them. Amen.*

311 Monday of the Second Week of the Year

Heb 5:1-10; 1 Sam 15:16-23; Mark 2:18-22

> *Help the weak ones that cry for help, help the prosecuted and the victim . . . they are the comrades that fight and fall . . . for the conquest of the joy of freedom for all the poor workers. In this struggle for life you will find more love and you will be loved.*
>
> (Nicola Sacco, *Letter to His son Dante*)

> *. . . un Cristo agonizante*
> *símbolo eterno del tormento humano.*
> (Ricardo Jaimes Freyre, "Hoc Signum," *Antología,* Onis 368)

Before Vatican Council II, Catholics were taught to engage in many "supererogatory" works, such as, fasting, extra prayers, and sacrifices. We must admit that these practices betrayed a certain rigidity and legislation and even a disparagement of the body. Today's readings show us a different aspect. Our practices reflect the ways we conceive God. A judgmental God will require expiation, sacrifices, fasting, a disciplining of the body. A special class of persons may be set aside to perform sacred duties on behalf of the "less worthy" members. But a benign, even jovial, God is less likely to inspire such works. Each individual has within themselves the ability to offer spiritual sacrifices in accordance with their image of God. The reading from Hebrews shows Jesus' transcending the levitical type of priesthood which involved much ritual purity, and the offering of many and varied sacrifices. It was an exclusively male priesthood. The author of Hebrews predicates of Jesus another kind of priesthood, that of Melchizedek. Melchizedek is found in Genesis 14 where Abraham offers him tithes and Melchizedek brings out bread and wine. He is also met in Psalm 110 which presents him as priest-king. Traditions about Melchizedek were multifarious and varied but most agreed that he was a supernatural (not divine) figure and probably offered bloodless sacrifices, like bread and wine. They thought of him as ushering in the year of good favor for the chosen people. In the second reading, Samuel tells Saul that God wishes people to listen to the divine call rather than offer animal sacrifices. In the third reading, Jesus emphasizes that there are times when fasting is not appropriate: we should not become ensconced in inflexible routine acts of self-discipline.

Jesus is a high priest full of compassion and human empathy. The Christian who wrote this letter to the Hebrews treasured the image of God which is reflected in the following famous passage from Exodus: the context is Moses ascending to the mountain again to receive the second tablets of the Torah after the sin of the golden calf.

> *The Lord, the Lord, a merciful and gracious God, slow to anger and rich in kindness and fidelity, continuing his kindness for a thousand generations, and forgiving wickedness and crime and sin; yet not declaring the guilty guiltless. . . .* (Exod 34:6-7)

Intercessions

For the grace of flexibility;

For a religion which does not become a source of gain.

Prayer

Merciful God, Author of All Compassion,
forgive us that we have sullied your image within us.
Enable us to reflect your true glory in the world,
a glory of sensitivity, of forgiveness, of concern. Amen.

312   Tuesday of the Second Week of the Year

Heb 6:10-20; 1 Sam 16:1-13; Mark 2:23-28

Roll, years of promise, rapidly roll round,
Till not a slave shall on this earth be found.   (J. Q. Adams, *Poem*)

Mientras quede algo esclavo
no será mi alma libre,
ni Tú, Señor . . . .
(Miguel de Unamuno, "Libértate, Señor," *Antología*, Onis, 216)

An oath is a solemn undertaking and the reading from Hebrews shows that God took promises very seriously. He pledged descendants, land, and liberty to Abraham and Sarah and said that their seed would multiply like the stars of heaven or the sands of the sea. Throughout history God kept his oath, even if it was not exactly in the form that people expected. His commitment to Abraham and Sarah was fulfilled in David who conquered Israel's enemies, extended the boundaries of the Promised Land and gave birth to children who were ancestors of Jesus Christ. Very often God fulfilled promises through seemingly insignificant figures like the shepherd boy, David. Naturally, God had no need to confirm his word by an oath or promises but, as Philo says, "It was to convince created man (and woman) of his weakness and to accompany conviction with help and comfort" (Philo, cited by Attridge, 179). The oath undergirds God's immutability and constancy. Can we say that we have kept all our promises faithfully? Human inconstancy is mirrored in Juliet's words to Romeo:

(Romeo): Lady, by yonder blessèd moon I swear
That tips with silver all these fruit-tree tops—
(Juliet): O! swear not by the moon, the inconstant moon,
That monthly changes in her circled orb,
Lest that thy love prove likewise variable.

(Romeo and Juliet, 2.2.107)

Intercessions

That we may discern the Spirit of God in the "little people";

That no law may hinder our nourishing those who are physically and spiritually hungry.

Prayer

O God of Staunch Truth and Love-bound Constancy,
  forgive the frailty of our nature,
our fickle words and our boastful promises unfulfilled.
  Fortify us with the Spirit of Truth
that we be not like "surf tossed and driven by the wind" Amen.

313   Wednesday of the Second Week of the Year

Heb 7:1-3, 15-17; 1 Sam 17:32-33, 37, 40-51; Mark 3:1-6

While with an eye made quiet by the power
Of harmony, and the deep power of joy,
We see into the life of things.   (Wordsworth, *Tintern Abbey*)

Todo el que camina anda,
como Jesús, sobre el mar.

(Antonio Machado, "Proverbios y Cantares II,"
Antología, Onis, 281)

All three lessons speak of an intangible power which comes from God rather than human beings. Melchizedek is priest but not because he was born into a priestly tribe and inherited the priesthood. David, a mere shepherd boy, overcomes Goliath, the giant. Jesus, through some supernatural power, cures the man with the withered hand. The readings cause us to reflect on different aspects of power and their sources. The quotation from Wordsworth illustrates the power of harmony. But there is power also in knowledge (Bacon); in music

(Dryden), nonviolent resistance (Martin Luther King, Jr.); in beauty (Buonarroti) and in sisterhood (R. Morgan). It is no easy task to balance power and virtue. As Niebuhr says:

> Goodness, armed with power, is corrupted;
> and pure love without power is destroyed.
> (Reinhold Niebuhr, Beyond Tragedy)

Intercessions

> That we may come to know that "power of life which cannot be destroyed";
>
> That we may temper power with mercy.

Prayer

> God, omnipotent in your power of love,
>   by his cross your Son showed us the potency of the powerless.
> Help us to discern those secret sources of strength
>   which blend with your cosmic harmony. Amen.

314 Thursday of the Second Week of the Year

Heb 7:25–8:6; 1 Sam 18:6-9; 19:1-7; Mark 3:7-12

> True love's the gift which God has given
> To man alone beneath the heaven:
> It is not fantasy's hot fire,
> Whose wishes, soon as granted, fly;
> It liveth not in fierce desire,
> With dead desire it doth not die;
> It is the secret sympathy,
> The silver link, the silken tie,
> Which heart to heart and mind to mind
> In body and in soul can bind.
> (Sir Walter Scott, The Lay of the Last Minstrel)

> . . . alma mía . . .
> duerme en la vieja cuna
> de la esperanza . . . .
> (Miguel de Unamuno, "Duerme, Alma Mía," Antología, Onis, 217)

The key note to our readings is "intercession." In the first reading, we see the ministry of Jesus who, exalted to the majesty of God, intercedes for us and wins for us access to his heavenly status. Our salvation is complete in every sense. In the second, Jonathan pleads for the life of his friend, David. In the third reading, we see the people crowding round Jesus so that through his divine power they may be healed of their afflictions. Here his intercessory power is seen with reference to physical and social needs but in Hebrews with reference to spiritual needs and eternal life.

Jews and early Christians believed that many virtuous persons could intercede for them to God, especially the priests and martyrs, but for Christians the great intercessors were Jesus and the Holy Spirit. However, to be an intercessor one must have experiences similar to those for whom one prays. Thus Christ became the great intercessor in virtue of his human experience of joy and suffering. He might have thought like Tennyson:

> I am a part of all that I have met;
> Yet all experience is an arch wherethrough
> Gleams that untraveled world.   (Tennyson, *Ulysses*)

Intercessions

> That we might see experience as "a cluster of gifts."
> (Henry James)

> That it might give us the "power to guess the unseen from the seen."   (Henry James)

Prayer

> God, Molder of Pain and Joy,
>   help us to glean the fertile harvest of our experience
> so that we bond ourselves
>   with the joyful and sorrowful of this world. Amen.

315   Friday of the Second Week of the Year

Heb 8:6-13; 1 Sam 24:3-21; Mark 3:13-19

God give us men! A time like this demands
Strong minds, great hearts, true faith, and ready hands;
Men whom the lust of office does not kill;
Men whom the spoils of office cannot buy;
Men who possess opinions and a will;
Men who have honor; men who will not lie.

(J. G. Holland, *Wanted*)

Dios te conserve fría la cabeza,
caliente el corazón, la mano larga . . . .

(Miguel de Unamuno, "Redención," *Antología,* Onis, 220)

Our first lesson speaks about the new covenant which is not made on tablets of stone like those which Moses received. These were mainly negative commandments and can be paralleled in other ancient Near Eastern legal codes. This new covenant, or bonding with God and humankind, springs from the depth of the heart. It is not guided by external, written rules and regulations but is prompted by the Holy Spirit to aspire even beyond the letter of the law. David could have killed King Saul—according to the contemporary culture this was permissible—but he saved his life and won reconciliation with the man who had sought to kill him. Great is the power of forgiveness.

Intercessions

That we may be kind to our enemies;

That we may know our true calling by Christ.

Prayer

Gentle and merciful God, your joy is ever to forgive
and to leap beyond the stricture of human law.
Grant us that inward flexibility,
tempered by the delicate breath of the Spirit,
which lifts us aloft to heroic love. Amen.

316　Saturday of the Second Week of the Year

Heb 9:2-3, 11-14; 2 Sam 1:1-4, 11-12, 19, 23-27; Mark 3:20-21

Who are these coming to the sacrifice?
To what green altar, O mysterious priest,
Lead'st thou that heifer lowing at the skies,
And all her silken flanks with garlands drest?

(Keats, *Ode on a Grecian Urn*)

Recibe como un santo sacramento
el perfume y la luz que te da el viento . . . .

(Francisco Villaespesa, "Humildad," *Antología*, 242)

Nearly all cultures have at times offered animal (and sometimes) human sacrifice to appease deities (gods and goddesses). Christ came to offer the sacrifice of his life not as a form of appeasement to an angry god, but as an act of friendship. In John's Gospel, Jesus says that there is no greater love than to lay one's life down for another (John 15:13). Therefore, Christ's voluntary sacrifice was an act of friendship which shows with amazing clarity what man and woman mean to God. They are God's friends. Cicero describes this bond as follows:

And yet love is further strengthened by the receiving of a kindly service, by the evidence of another's care for us, and by closer familiarity, and from all these, when joined to the soul's first impulse to love, there springs up, if I may say so, a marvelous glow and greatness of goodwill.　　(Cicero, *On Friendship*)

The second reading contains one of the most celebrated and moving lamentations over the death of friends in all literature. It is poignant because death through cruel and, often, senseless war is preeminently tragic. Yet to the person in antiquity it was also a source of honour. Men, macho men, loved war as is shown from the following quotation:

Let me have war, say I; it exceeds peace as far as day does night; it's sprightly, waking, audible, and full of vent. Peace is a very apoplexy, lethargy; mulled, deaf, sleepy, insensible; a getter of more bastard children than war's a destroyer of men.

(*Coriolanus*, 4.5.224–28)

Our world faces a different kind of war where the consequences, the destruction of humanity, land, sea, air, far outweigh the advantage of fighting. True war is of the Spirit, the war against poverty, ignorance, drugs and degradation. We can understand Jesus when he says that his kingdom is not of this world, if it were so, his supporters would fight to deliver him (John 18:36).

Intercessions

That we may know the true meaning of sacrifice;

That war might lose its attraction.

Prayer

Pacific God of Joy and Harmony,
* teach your people*
the elegant science of peacemaking.
* May we seek your kingdom in*
the dignity of the human person,
* the freedom of every state;*
*   the fair distribution of wealth*
*   and the sacred custody*
*   of the earth, sky and sea. Amen.*

68 Third Sunday of the Year
Cycle A

Isa 8:23–9:3; 1 Cor 1:10-13, 17; Matt 1:12-23 or 4:12-17

First of all the fisher should have body and limbs both swift and strong. . . . For often he must fight with mighty fish in landing them. . . . And lightly he must leap from a rock; and, when the toil of the sea is at its height, he must swiftly travel a long way and dive into the deepest depths and abide amongst the waves and remain labouring at such works as men upon the sea toil at with enduring heart.   (Oppian, *Halieutica*)

. . .
sé como el agua, dócil a la ley infinita,
que reza en las iglesias en donde está bendita,
y en el estanque arrulla meciendo la piragua.
    (Amado Nervo, "La Hermana Agua," *Antología*, Onis, 400)

The first and third reading speak of reverse of fortune. The northern tribes, Zebulun and Naphtali, were conquered by Assyria in the eighth century B.C.E. and the symbols of Assyrian power were the yoke, the staff and the rod. Isaiah speaks of Yahweh's victory and joy returning to the people. Nevertheless, pagan influences had already been sown in the north and some Jewish people never really overcame their antipathy towards the people in the Northern Kingdom, who were eventually denoted as "Samaritans" after the name of the capital of the Northern Kingdom. Rivalry between these two people lasted even into the days of the early church. But the Gospel shows Jesus bringing the gospel message to the northern people. So Jesus' ministry begins with an effort to unite two usually hostile groups. The second lesson also deals with conflicts.

To assist him in his ministry Jesus calls fishermen. They were probably from a group of middle-class fish traders, not from the lowest social class.[7] Theirs was an important trade because for the majority of people fish was the principal item of their diet, next to bread, and also the rich sought gourmet fish for their sumptuous banquets. The fisherman had to be not only physically robust but also possessed of "cunning of wit and wise" and "daring and dauntless and temperate, wakeful of heart and open-eyed" (Oppian, *Halieutica*). Further, people would understand when Jesus spoke about the disciples becoming "fishers of human beings." Philosophers in the ancient world used this idea, e.g., Plato uses a similar metaphor when discussing teacher-student relationships. For example, in the *Sophist* he says:

> Now up to that point the sophist and the angler proceed together from the starting-point of acquisitive art. . . . But the other (the fisher of human persons, not animals) turns toward the land and to rivers of a different kind—rivers of wealth and youth, bounteous meadows, as it were—and he intends to coerce the creatures in them.

In the Bible God is also portrayed as a fisher (e.g., Job 10:16; 19:6). So Jesus chose persons with plenty of "spunk" and shrewdness and these abilities were to be used also in their missionary work.

Intercessions

> That we might not disdain the use of wisdom
> and the skills of this world in our apostolate;

[7]Readers will find much information about this topic in W. H. Wuellner, *The Meaning of "Fishers of Men,"* (Philadelphia: Westminster Press, 1967).

That we may strive to be of one heart within our communities.

Prayer

O God, True Angler and Hunter of Humankind,
search for us in the turbulent sea
of our conflicting desires.
Allure us with the bait of your love
and capture us in the net of your felicity. Amen.

69 Third Sunday of the Year
Cycle B

Jonah 3:1-5, 10; 1 Cor 7:29-31; Mark 1:14-20

Procrastination is the thief of time.
(Edward Young, *Night Thoughts*)

Vuelve hacia atrás la vista, caminante,
verás lo que te queda de camino . . . .
(Miguel de Unamuno, "Vuelve hacia atrás la Vista,"
Antología, Onis, 229)

Today's readings are urgent in character. For Jonah there are only forty days and Nineveh will be destroyed or, as some would read it, "turned over," that is, have a change of mind. Paul expects the second coming of Jesus very soon and Jesus calls the fishermen to radical discipleship, that is, to surrender immediately home, employment and family to follow him and proclaim the Kingdom. There could be no procrastination. Indeed, an alternative reading to "forty days" in the Jonah text is "three days" which increases the urgency. Further, when Luke discusses radical discipleship he represents Jesus as requiring that those who follow him should not delay even to bid farewell to their families or bury their dead (Luke 9:57-62). Are we dilatory with regard to Christ's kingdom?

Intercessions

For greater generosity in discipleship;
For punctility in gratitude and love.

Prayer

> *Limitless Source of Joy and Clarity,*
> *inject the gaiety of your Spirit*
> *into the flatness of our pedestrian life.*
> *Ignite our souls so that*
> *our felicity be so contagious,*
> *that it may quicken all that it touches. Amen.*

70 Third Sunday of the Year
Cycle C

Neh 8:1-4a, 5-6, 8-10; 1 Cor 12:12-30 or 12:12-14, 27; Lk 1:1-4, 14-21

> *They say, best men are moulded out of faults;*
> *And, for the most, become much more the better*
> *For being a little bad. . . .*
>
> (Shakespeare, *Measure for Measure*, 5.1.435-37)

> *Las manos sacralmente*
> *tomaron esos panes rojizos, lenguas vivas,*
> *e impusieron su forma.*
>
> (Vicente Aleixandre, "La Obra del Albañil," *Los Derechos*, 348)

The readings today emphasize the role of the people of God. In the first lesson Ezra shares the Torah or God's revelation with the people. Some scholars suggest that this was the first time that the Torah was read in the vernacular so that all might understand. The second lesson stresses the importance of the ministries of the Spirit by all members of the community. Paul takes a well-known simile, used by classical writers to illustrate the unity of a city, and he applies it to the Christian community. All members are one and all are important in the resurrected body of Christ. In the third reading Jesus, as an ordinary town citizen, proclaims the gospel to all, Jew and Gentile alike, for in quoting the text from Isaiah Jesus omits the reference to vengeance on the Gentiles. Further, it is to be noted that the ''little people'' play an important part in the Gospels themselves. In Mark, for example, the apostles appear obtuse, faithless, cowardly and lacking in perseverance, whereas the little people like the two blind men, the blind man at Bethsaida (Mark 8:22-26) and Bartimaeus (Mark 10:15-52) not only respond with faith and alacrity to Jesus but they symbolize the dawning and the attaining of pure faith. They represent the adherents to the "new covenant" predicted by Jeremiah:

> But this is the covenant which I will make with the house of Israel after those days, says the Lord. I will place my law within them, and write it upon their hearts; I will be their God, and they shall be my people. No longer will they have need to teach their friends and kinsmen how to know the Lord, All, from least to greatest, shall know me, says the Lord. . . . (Jer 31:33-34)

Intercessions

> For a full appreciation of the ministries of each person in the community;
>
> For those physically and those spiritually blind.

Prayer

> You, who are the Discerner of All Hearts,
>   whose Son became an insignificant babe
> whom many held in no esteem.
>   We beg you,
> never let us miss
>   treasures hidden in earthen vessels. Amen.

317 Monday of the Third Week of the Year

Heb 9:15, 24-28; 2 Sam 5:1-7, 10; Mark 3:22-30

> Rise up, O hero!
> Lead off Thy captives, O Glorious One!
> Gather up Thy spoils, O Author of mighty deeds!
> (From a prayer in the War Scroll, Column 12, Dead Sea Scrolls)

> Venga a nos, no tu reino, tu figura
> en forma de piedad y no de celo.
>   (Arturo Serrano Plaja, "Padre Nuestro," Antología, Cano, 95)

The second and third lessons speak of "kingdoms." In the Samuel text, the people choose David because he is bone of their bone and flesh of their flesh; Adam uses the same expression when God presents

Eve to him. Under David the kingdom of the Jewish people spread more extensively than under any other sovereign. David was an assertive and impulsive king although one who was highly sensitive to the needs of his people. He was also humble before God and was ready to take responsibility for the sins he committed. In the gospel reading, Jesus speaks about a different kind of kingdom, the dominion of Satan. He points out that if he were working through Satan, he would certainly not be casting out demons for that would destroy Satan's kingdom. One can see the two kingdoms of good and evil in conflict in a unique document from the Dead Scrolls. This is called the *War Scroll of the Sons of Light against the Son of Darkness:* it is a battle between Satan, his angels and wicked people against God, his angels and good people. If Jesus were on the side of the Sons of Darkness then he would not be destroying Satan. Further, Jesus mentions the "unforgivable sin." This is patient of many interpretations but it appears to mean attributing the ministry of Jesus to Satan and not to the Holy Spirit. Jesus is the stronger person who has entered Satan's domain and tied him up as prisoner. Jesus' kingdom is the firm establishment of good over evil.

Intercessions

That we may eagerly await salvation;

That we may be able to recognize the work of the Spirit.

Prayer

Covenant God,
 you hung your war bow upside down in the sky.
You made a covenant with Noah, his family and all living creatures
 that the world should not be destroyed by flood again.
Grant us to remember our covenant
 with our sisters and brothers,
so that we set aside our weapons of destruction
 and preserve their lives. Amen.

318 Tuesday of the Third Week of the Year

Heb 10:1-10; 2 Sam 6:12-15, 17-19; Mark 3:31-35

Forasmuch as God has given to thee (Hector) as to none other works of war, therefore in counsel too art thou minded to have wisdom beyond all; but in no wise shalt thou be able of thine own self to compass all things. To one man hath God given works of war, to another the dance, to another the lyre and song, and in the breast of another Zeus, whose voice is born afar, putteth a mind of understanding, wherefrom many may get profit. . . .

(Homer, *Iliad*)

. . . me río
porque es una forma de pudor la risa . . . .
(Luis G. Urbina, "Confesión," *Antología*, Onís, 424)

These three texts are rich indeed and it is difficult to select the best theme. The reader may find my choice surprising. I have selected the image of David dancing before the ark of God. Many non-Western cultures employ all the senses and emotions and use "body language" to communicate with God and the community. Dance is part of that body language. In Hebrew culture it was an expression of gladness and sometimes reached the pitch of religious ecstasy: this is particularly true of the very early prophets. The *Encyclopaedia Judaica* (New York: Macmillan, 1971 [5:1262-71]) points out that the Bible has eleven verbs to describe dance movements and that this points to "an advanced stage of choreography among the Jews." Five of these are employed in our present text with reference to David and the people dancing before the Lord. They mean "to dance"; "to rotate with all his might"; "to jump"; "to skip"; other words for the same activity in the Hebrew Bible mean "jump with both feet," "to turn around," "limp" and "dance in a circle." Occasions for such demonstrative behavior were wooing and weddings; victory; nature dances; harvest and vineyard dances; sabbath dances; ecstatic prophetic dances; dances on the occasions of circumcision and memorials, e.g. in honor of revered teachers. Perhaps we need more body language and freedom when we worship our God of gladness and strive to build up self and community. The Spanish writer, Pablo Neruda (1904–1973) wrote:

All paths lead to the same goal: to convey to others what we are. And we must pass through solitude and difficulty, isolation and silence, in order to reach forth to the enchanted place where we

can dance our clumsy dance and sing our sorrowful song—but in
this dance or in this song there are fulfilled the most ancient rites
of our conscience in the awareness of being human and of believ-
ing in a common destiny.

(*Toward the Splendid City*, upon receiving the
Nobel Prize, 1971)

Intercessions

For relaxation in God's presence;

For entertainers that their art may please God and build up com-
munity.

Prayer

God, our Creator,
  you crafted the human body
with meticulous care and unstinted love.
  May we never desecrate
these temples of your Spirit.
  May they express our exuberant joy
in your presence. Amen.

319 Wednesday of the Third Week of the Year

Heb 10:11-18; 2 Sam 7:4-17; Mark 4:1-20

Sow a thought, and you reap an act;
Sow an act, and you reap a habit;
Sow a habit, and you reap a character;
Sow a character, and you reap a destiny.

(Anonymous, quoted by Samuel Smiles in *Life and Labor*)

. . .

el Dios adusto de la tierra parda.

(Antonia Machado, "El Dios Ibero," *Antología*, Onis, 271)

Commentators on the well known parable of the Sower often speak
about the seed and the farmer but not so frequently about the earth
herself. Here is a hymn to Earth, the Mother of All, by the Greek epic

poet, Hesiod. It should be meaningful to us in these days of ecological awareness.

> *I will sing of well-founded Earth, mother of all, oldest of all be-ings. She feeds all creatures that are in the world, all that go upon the goodly land, and all that are in the paths of the sea, and all that fly: all these are fed of her store. Through you, O queen, men (and women) are blessed in their children and blessed in their har-vests, and to you it belongs to give means of life to mortal men (and women) and to take it away. Happy is the man (or woman) whom you delight to honour! He has all things abundantly: his fruitful land is laden with corn, his pastures are covered with cattle, and his house is filled with good things. Such men rule orderly in their cities of fair women; great riches and wealth follow them; their sons exult with everfresh delight, and their daughters with flower-laden bands play and skip merrily over the soft flowers of the field. Thus is it with those whom you honour, O holy god-dess, bountiful spirit. Hail, Mother of the gods, wife of starry Heaven; freely bestow upon me for this my song substance that cheers the heart!* (Hesiod, *Homeric Hymns*)

Although Jesus did not see the earth as a goddess yet he must have been close to nature and appreciated especially her harvest gifts of field and sea. For him the kingdom of God could be likened to the earth and the seed which farmers sowed in her. The Jewish people treas-ured the land, insisted that she should have her sabbaths (fallow years) and that she should not be polluted but cared for. They believed the land would "vomit them out" if they desecrated her.

Intercessions

> *For the faith and humility of David;*
> *For our mother, the earth.*

Prayer

> *Bountiful God, you are lavish with your gifts,*
>   *both material and spiritual.*
> *Help us to be true stewards of your kingdom.*
>   *May we be wise and generous in our sowing,*
> *gentle and greedless in our reaping,*
>   *and just in our distribution of your bounty. Amen.*

320   Thursday of the Third Week of the Year

Heb 10:19-25; 2 Sam 7:18-19, 24-29; Mark 4:21-25

Earth's crammed with heaven,
And every common bush afire with God.

(E. B. Browning, *Aurora Leigh*)

. . .

que funde las palabras de mi lengua
y las hace de miel y de fragancia . . . .
(Roberto Brenes Mesén, "Cálmame, Señor," *Antología*, Onis 751)

Most religions have boundaries which mark off the sacred and the profane (secular). This is true with regard to personal and worship spaces. The Hebrew religion was no exception. It gradually developed a special class of priests and levites to serve in the Temple and drew up certain rules for worship and daily life. But these boundaries also classified people so that certain groups were excluded and often despised, such as women, slaves, the handicapped and people of other religious persuasions. Our passage from Hebrews shows that all this has been superseded. The author of Hebrews speaks of the average human person gaining access to the very presence of God through their common humanity with Jesus. Now there is no Greek or Jew, no male or female, no free person or slave, no handicapped but all are one and equal in Christ (cf. Gal 3:28). Unfortunately, the Church has not always implemented this teaching of Jesus and of the Epistle to the Hebrews. She formed a clerical class, exclusive ritual and a penitential system. However, we live in hopeful times which may see a return of the priesthood for all the laity. The second reading speaks about the dynasty of King David, who was a "lay" person, not a priest. Jesus was born from his dynasty. The third reading speaks of the hidden lamps, an eloquent symbol for unrecognized lay persons, especially women in the church today.

Intercessions

That we may not hide our lights under bushel baskets;

That we may know the mystery of drawing nearer to God.

Prayer

Jesus, Our Brother,
you have taught us to multiply our talents.

Let us not begrudge the gifts of others,
  thinking that thereby ours will shine with greater glamour.
Let us know how brightly
"shines a good deed in a naughty world." Amen.

321 Friday of the Third Week of the Year

Heb 10:32-39; 2 Sam 11:1-4, 5-10, 13-17; Mark 4:26-34

For peace, with justice and honor, is the fairest and most profit-
able of possessions, but with disgrace and shameful cowardice it
is the most infamous and harmful of all.

(Polybius, *Histories*, 4:31).

Y tu "carrera"
al hombre enseña, al fin, de qué manera
puede ser Dios un condenado a muerte.
(Manuel Machado, "Jesus del Gran Poder," *Los Derechos*, 256)

The first and second readings intimate the theme of cowardice. The
Epistle to the Hebrews tells us that God takes no pleasure in the person who "draws back" and 2 Samuel shows David as a man unable
to face his paternal responsibility and even stooping to callous murder to evade it. It is a curious thing but cowardice and cruelty are often
combined. Let me give some examples. Thomas Malory says "Ever
will a coward show no mercy" (*Morte d'Arthur*); and Michel de Mon-
taigne (*Essays*) states that "Cowardice is the mother of cruelty." This
we see, indeed, in the case of David, brave as a warrior, cowardly as
a father and adulterer. Similarly, C. S. Lewis represents the senior devil
Screwtape saying to junior devil Wormwood: "Hatred is best combined
with Fear. Cowardice, alone of all the vices, is purely painful—horrible
to anticipate, horrible to feel, horrible to remember; Hatred has its
pleasures. It is therefore often the *compensation* by which a frightened
man reimburses himself of the miseries of Fear. The more he fears,
the more he will hate" (*The Screwtape Letters*). But Lewis also gives us
some encouragement:

All the rabbit in us is to disappear—the worried, conscientious,
ethical rabbit as well as the cowardly and sensual rabbit. We shall
bleed and squeal as the handfuls of fur come out; and then, sur-
prisingly, we shall find underneath it all a thing we have never

yet imagined: a real Man, an ageless god, a son of God, strong,
radiant, wise, beautiful, and drenched in joy.

(God in the Dock)

Intercessions

For patience and gentleness in suffering,

For the base Christian communities
which may be the mustard seed of the church.

Prayer

O God, your Son showed courage in the face of
rejection, ridicule and death.
When our weak human nature cringes with fear
transfuse us with his valor. Amen.

322 Saturday of the Third Week of the Year

Heb 11:1-2, 8-19; 2 Sam 12:1-7, 10-17; Mark 4:35-41

Humor is a prelude to faith and laughter is the beginning of prayer.
(Reinhold Niebuhr, *Discerning the Signs of the Times*)

Oración campesina
que temblaba en la azul
santidad matutina.

(Ramón del Valle-Inclán, "Milagro de la Mañana,"
Antología, Onis, 326)

Some confuse "faith" with a confidence that miracles will be performed. Others tend to identify "faith" with a belief in a literal interpretation of the Scriptures. But in reality often mature faith cannot exist
save in adversity. Often it is preceded by doubt. Thus in the gospel
lesson, the disciples exhibit their faith by calling upon Jesus when they
are in need. They may not have expected a miraculous intervention.
Perhaps they just needed another hand to bale out the water or steer
or row the boat. The parents of faith are perplexity and trial. Faith is
a quiet confidence mingled with wisdom and hope. Thus Hebrews'
definition of faith is superb: "Faith is confident assurance concerning
what we hope for, and conviction about things we do not see" (Heb
11:1). C. S. Lewis said:

If we wish to be rational, not now and then, but constantly, we must pray for the gift of Faith, for the power to go on believing not in the teeth of reason but in the teeth of lust and terror and jealousy and boredom and indifference that which reason, authority, or experience, or all three, have once delivered to us for truth.   (Christian Reflections)

But faith need not be colorless. George Sand (a pseudonym, for she was a woman) draws our attention to this:

Faith is an excitement and an enthusiasm: it is a condition of intellectual magnificence to which we must cling as to a treasure, and not squander . . . in the small coin of empty words. . . .
                                (George Sand, Letter to Des Planches)

Intercessions

For a just relationship between rich and poor;

For integrity in courts of law.

Prayer

God, Our Bond Fellow,
*   you gave us the example of Jesus*
as the pioneer of our faith.
*   Strip from us all that might be called*
superstition, not faith,
*   and conceive within us*
the vibrancy of confidence
*   in divine and human persons. Amen.*

71   Fourth Sunday of the Year
Cycle A

Zeph 2:3; 3:12-13; 1 Cor 1:26-31; Matt 5:1-12

We're never single-minded, unperplexed, like migratory birds.
(Rainer Maria Rilke, The Duino Elegies)

La mentira me tiene
amordazado . . . .

> (Rafael Montesinos, "Tres Canciones sobre la Verdad,"
> *Los Derechos,* 254)

The first and third readings speak of innocence, honesty, single-heartedness. The comparison with a migratory bird (above) is apt. She flies unerringly to her chosen spot, every sense used to direct her course, braving every element which might hinder her. Similarly Samuel Johnson said: "To dread no eye, and to suspect no tongue, is the greatest prerogative of innocence" (The Rambler). Jesus himself told his disciples to be as innocent as doves and wise as serpents. But innocence is not goodness itself but the fertile ground for the fruits of the Spirit. These fruits are reflected in the beatitudes, single-heartedness, seeking righteousness, showing mercy and creating peace.

Intercessions

For an understanding of God's foolishness;

For respect for the powerless.

Prayer

God of Sacred Truth,
  teach us the enormity of every form of deceit,
whether in private or public domain,
  with friend or foe.
Let us be true disciples of your Son,
  who is the Way, the Truth and the Life. Amen.

72 Fourth Sunday of the Year
Cycle B

Deut 18:18-20; 1 Cor 7:32-35; Mark 1:21-28

R. Aibu said that when Adam sinned, the Shechinah withdrew to the first (and lowest) heaven, when Cain sinned to the second, in the generations of Enoch to the third, in the generations of the flood to the fourth, in the generation of the Dispersion of Tongues to the fifth, through the sin of men of Sodom to the sixth, and through the sin of the Egyptians to the seventh [and highest] heaven. Then six righteous men arose, and they brought the Shechinah back to the earth. For Abraham brought it back to the sixth heaven, Isaac to the fifth, Jacob to the fourth, Levi to the third, Kehat to the second, and Amram to the first. Moses finally brought it back from the upper world to the lower world [i.e. to earth]. For indeed the wicked cause the Shechinah to ascend from the earth, while the righteous cause it to dwell on the earth. When exactly did the Shechinah come down upon the earth? On the day when the Sanctuary was set up, as it is said, "Then the cloud covered the tent of meeting, and the glory of the Lord filled the Sanctuary." (Exod. xi, 34, Numbers Rabbah)

. . .

me mecen como al mar
mecen las dos orillas
el Angel que da el gozo
y el que da la agonía,
el de alas tremolantes
y el de las alas fijas.
(Gabriel Mistral, "Dos Angeles," *Once Grandes,* 187)

I have quoted at length because the above reflection is very powerful. The Shechinah is the radiant presence of God, the divine immanence in distinction from the divine transcendence. The root of the word means to "reside," "dwell," or "rest." In the Hebrew Scriptures the Spirit is always feminine. Later, about the beginning of the Christian era, the Jewish people developed the idea of the Shekinah or Spirit as the feminine aspect of the deity. She revealed the compassionate, merciful, nourishing, forgiving aspect of God. The mystics developed the idea of the Shechinah still more and spoke of her going into exile with Israel, weeping when they suffered, rejoicing when they prospered. However, the Jews were very careful not to portray her as a goddess. Various concepts are linked to the Shekinah, especially those of light and glory. She is also associated with charismatic persons as the above quotation suggests. Moses is shown as the true prophet who brings the presence of God, or the Shekinah, down to earth.

It is within our power to draw the Shekinah into our world or to impede her presence. This is an alarming realization.

Intercessions

That we may heed the prophetesses of God;

That we may disencumber ourselves from needless anxieties.

Prayer

> O God, you are our Father and our Mother,
>   let us not shrink from declaring your maternity
> or resist the bonds of love
>   with which you draw us. Amen.

73 Fourth Sunday of the Year
Cycle C

Jer 1:4-5, 17-19; 1 Cor 12:31–13:13 or 13:4-13; Luke 4:21-30

> A prophet comforts the afflicted
>   and afflicts the comfortable.

> Viento de profecía
> que a las tinieblas del vivir envía
> la evangélica luz de un nuevo día.
>> (Enrique González Martínez, "Viento Sagrado,"
>> Antología, Onis, 496)

The first lesson tells us of the call of the prophet, Jeremiah, who lived in the sixth century when Babylon threatened and finally conquered Judah. At this time many of the people, especially the leaders, went into exile. Jeremiah met much opposition. He tried to confront the people and the religious leaders with their faults but suffered grievously as a consequence. We see a similar situation in the gospel lesson, where Jesus scandalizes the people because he speaks favorably of the Gentiles (the nonJewish nations) who were often the enemies of the Jews. A prophet is always a threat especially when he or she comes from the community itself. We might think of a similar American prophet, Martin Luther King, Jr., or Oscar Romero, representative of so many prophets who confront both church and state in Latin America. In the gospel reading, we see Jesus as a prophet whom his own town folk not only rejected but attempted to assassinate. The lesson from Paul describes the kind of love and commitment which every prophet should possess.

Intercessions

That we might have the wisdom and the courage for confrontation;

That we might receive a harvest of the fruits of love.

Prayer

God of the Prophetic Spirit,
  teach us that prophets and prophetesses
within our communities
  must confront as well as console,
destroy inappropriate attitudes
  as well as build appropriate ones,
even as did your Son, Jesus of Nazareth. Amen.

323 Monday of the Fourth Week of the Year

Heb 11:32-40; 2 Sam 15, 13-14, 30; 16:5-13

Where there is charity and wisdom, there is neither fear nor igno-
rance. Where there is patience and humility, there is neither anger
nor vexation. Where there is poverty and joy, there is neither greed
nor avarice. Where there is peace and meditation, there is neither
anxiety nor doubt.

(St. Francis of Assisi, *The Counsels of*
the Holy Father St. Francis)

Nacimos crucificados
como los largos senderos.

(Ángel Cruchaga Santa María, ''Los Hijos de Job,''
Antología, Onis, 781)

All three readings address the subject of faith in different ways. In
the Hebrews' reading, we have a list of noble men and women who
kept their faith with God in spite of appalling circumstances. In 2
Samuel, David submits himself to humiliation and patient waiting on
God even though his own son rises against him and one of his own
people curses him. A curse was greatly feared in the ancient world
and this throws David's faith into even higher relief. In the gospel reading, Jesus cures a wild madman and then informally commissions him
to spread the news of the faith: the man represents the downtrodden

of humanity who often externalize their fears, oppression and needs for bare subsistence level of living by unconventional behavior. It is our responsibility to cultivate the fruits of the Spirit so that these circumstances do not arise.

Prayer (attributed to St. Francis)

> Lord, make me an instrument of Your peace,
>   Where there is hatred let me sow love;
> where there is injury, pardon;
>   where there is doubt, faith;
> where there is despair, hope;
>   where there is darkness, light;
> and where there is sadness, joy;
> O divine Master,
>   grant that I may not so much seek
> to be consoled as to console;
>   to be understood as to understand;
> to be loved as to love.
> For it is in giving that we receive;
>   it is in pardoning that we are pardoned;
> and it is in dying
>   that we are born to eternal life. Amen.

324 Tuesday of the Fourth Week of the Year

Heb 12:1-4; 2 Sam 18:9-10, 14, 24-25, 30-19:3; Mark 5:21-43

A heavenly race demands thy zeal,/ And an immortal crown.
                                        (P. Doddridge, *Hymns*)

. . . ¡El alma es un vaso
que sólo se llena con eternidad!
                        (Amado Nervo, "La Sed," *Antología*, Onis, 413)

Once again we have the theme of faith. As the passage from Hebrews—the grande finale of the great encomium on faith—so aptly describes it, we are surrounded by a "cloud of witnesses." Jesus is the climax and epitome of all the examples of faith in the author's catalogue of faithful ones from Jewish history. However, of interest is the athletic imagery employed by the writer. As Harold Attridge (Harold

W. Attridge, *Hebrews*, Hermeneia [Philadelphia: Fortress Press, 1989] 354) observes ''cloud'' (*nephos*) in classical literature can mean a ''crowd,'' e.g. a cloud of footmen or of infantry; ''witnesses'' (*martyres*) can mean ''spectators.'' So the word ''cloud'' sets the athletic, contest imagery. We are, as it were, seated in a stadium. The Christians are bidden to remove any encumbrance like the athletes who stripped for a contest. The Christians are competitors in the race or battle of life. They are to run as if in a marathon. As they run, the Christians keep their eyes on their model, Jesus.

Here is part of the description of the foot race run to celebrate the funeral of Patroclus (*Iliad*). The son of Peleus set out the prizes, a mixing bowl, an ox and half a talent of gold.

> And he stood up and spake a word among the Argives: "Rise, ye who will essay this match." Thus spake he, and straightway arose fleet Aias Oileus' son, and Odysseus of many wiles, and after them Nestor's son Antilochos, for he was best of all the youth in the foot race. Then they stood side by side, and Achilles showed to them the goal. Right eager was the running from the start, but Oileus' son forthwith shot to the front, and close behind him came noble Odysseus, as close as is a weaving rod to a fair-girdled woman's breast when she pulleth it deftly with her hands, drawing the spool along the warp, and holdeth the rod nigh her breast, so close ran Odysseus behind Aias and trod in his footsteps or ever the dust had settled there, and on his head fell the breath of noble Odysseus as he ran ever lightly on, and all the Achaians applauded his struggle for the victory and called on him as he laboured hard. But when they were running the last part of the course forthwith Odysseus prayed in his soul to bright-eyed Athene: "Hearken, goddess, come thou a good helper of my feet." Thus prayed he, and Pallas Athene hearkened to him, and made his limbs feel light, both feet and hands. . . . So much-enduring noble Odysseus, as he came in first, took up the mixing bowl, and famous Aias took the ox. . . . Then Antilochus smiling bore off the last prize, and spake his word among the Argives: "Friends, ye will all bear me witness when I say that even herein also the immortals favour elder men. For Aias is a little older than I, but Odysseus of an earlier generation and earlier race of men. A green old age is his, they say, and hard were it for any Achaian to rival him in speed, save only Achilles."

What prize would we set out? How should we shed our *impediments*, how would we run the race?

Intercessions

For athletes, that they may use their gifts for God;
For the handicapped.

Prayer

God of Strength,
  you formed us as athletes in the contest of life.
Teach to shed the incumbrances of life;
  to run our course with fleet and surefooted endurance.
May the spectators of our world
  be kindled with our enthusiasm.
Let our eyes be raised to the goal, which is love incarnate. Amen.

325   Wednesday of the Fourth Week of the Year

Heb 12:4-7; 11-15; 2 Sam 24:2, 9-17; Mark 6:1-6

Men reject their prophets and slay them, but they love their mar-
tyrs and honor those whom they have slain.
                              (Dostoevski, *The Brothers Karamazou*)

Mi madre, dulce voz,
decía: "La verdad es norte de la vida."
                              (Juan Ruiz Peña, "Libertad," *Antología*, Cano, 197)

In the gospel reading, we find a typical socio-anthropological situation. The critic who appears among his own people is generally op-
posed, often ostracized, sometimes killed. There are many examples
from the secular and religious history. It was the fate of most of the
classical Hebrew prophets to be rejected or even murdered by their
own people, e.g. Jeremiah and Ezekiel. This is true also of many of
the philosophers, e.g. Socrates. As Wordsworth wrote:

Strongest minds
Are often those of whom the noisy world
Hears least.   (Wordsworth, *Excursion*)

Nevertheless, rejection brings its own consolations. Willa S. Cather
wrote:

Only solitary men know the full joys of friendship. Others have their family; but to a solitary and an exile his friends are everything. (Shadows on the Rock)

Intercessions

That familiarity may not breed contempt;

That political leaders may have the grace to acknowledge their mistakes.

Prayer

O God, you elected the shepherd boy, David,
in preference to his brothers.
Enable us to look, not at outward appearance,
but at the heart. Amen.

326   Thursday of the Fourth Week of the Year

Heb 12:18-19, 21-24; 1 Kgs 2:1-4, 10-12; Mark 6:7-13

Fear the earthly tribunal, even though witnesses against you can be bribed; fear yet more the heavenly tribunal, for pure witnesses will testify against you there, and, moreover, they proclaim continually, ''If you have fulfilled my words with joy, my servant will come to greet you, and I myself will go forth to meet you, and say to you, May your coming be in peace.''
(Derekh Erez Zuta 4:6)

¡Oh dulce Galilea, tanto recuerdo abrigas
en tu seno sagrado, que eres como un altar!
(Luis Felipe Contardo, "Misterium Sacrum," *Antología*, Onis 647)

The first and third readings speak of the Christians' new freedom in Jesus, the mediator of the New Covenant. The writer of Hebrews has been exhorting his readers to seek peace and holiness (Heb 12:14). In this passage he describes, as it were, a new Exodus. But now the people do not come from Egypt, arrive at a mountain and experience God amidst terrifying electrical storms and volcanoes. They are not excluded from the privileged place enjoyed by Moses, who does ascend the mountain. No, they approach the new Mount Zion, the new Jerusalem, "the ultimate point of God's manifestation" (Attridge, 374) to gather in festivity, one with celestial beings and the departed faithful. In a similar way the twelve disciples go forth on their first mission for Jesus with quiet confidence, implicit joy, travelling lightly and anticipating hospitality and help from those to whom they preach. They also have the freedom to "shake the dust off their feet," that is, to leave others the freedom to accept or reject the gospel message. They are not to harass people. Their mission is to free the enslaved—those enslaved by "demons," oppressive social and psychological burdens—and to heal the sick. As God redeemed the children of Israel from slavery in Egypt so now the disciples are given a chance to redeem others.

Intercessions

For the grace to "travel light";

For inspiration for those who, like David, take leave of life.

Prayer

Redeemer of the Chosen People,
  we pray you,
accomplish once more your mighty deeds.
  Free those under oppressive governments;
release your people from prison and torture;
  dissolve the panic
which prepares weapons of cosmic destruction.
  Heal the gentle earth
raped by human greed. Amen.

327 Friday of the Fourth Week of the Year

Heb 13:1-8; Sir 47:2-11; Mark 6:14-29

A good conscience is a continual feast.
                    (Robert Burton, *Anatomy of Melancholy,*
                              Democritus to the reader)

Me acerqué a la fiesta del mundo. Me puse
mi traje de fiesta.
Cuando yo llegaba,
estaban cerrando las puertas.
                    (Arturo Capdevila, "Me Acerqué a la Fiesta,"
                              Antología, Onis, 763)

The three readings focus on three themes: marriage; feasting (cf. David adding "beauty to the feasts" in the second reading); and imprisonment. Hebrews exhorts its readers: to practice hospitality (and in so doing it makes a reference to Abraham and Sarah who entertained three persons, later identified as angels), to keep chaste within marriage and to remember the imprisoned. But it is the gospel lesson which throws these themes into high relief. King Herod, whose marriage was incestuous, gives a great feast for his birthday. Feasts in the Roman world were often wildly extravagant and the dinner itself was accompanied by expensive entertainment, e.g., dancing and music. John, who rebuked Herod for his marital status, is in prison. Prisons were normally for those who were being retained for trial or execution. Conditions within them were notorious. They were dark, stifling, airless and overrun with rats and other vermin. The prisoners often wore shackles on their necks, arms and feet and were chained to a post, often with a short tie. So the gospel reading presents us with the levity and luxury of the court of Herod and the horrendous situation of John, Jesus' forerunner. He received a summary execution without any due process. The experience of John is not dissimilar to the situation of many in concentration camps nowadays. Here is an extract from Alexander Solzhenitsyn's novel, *One Day in the Life of Ivan Denisovich*, (New York: Signet Classic, 1962) which describes the dastardly condition of prisoners in Siberia. The prisoners lived on bread and fish soup, were compelled to hard labour in a temperature well below zero (minus seventeen to minus forty degrees), ill treated, deprived and summarily punished without any resource to justice. Yet the book ends thus:

> *Shukhov went to sleep fully content. He'd had many strokes of luck that day: they hadn't put him in the cells; they hadn't sent his squad to the settlement; he'd swiped a bowl of kasha (black cabbage) at dinner; the squad leader had fixed the rates well; he's built a wall and enjoyed doing it; he'd smuggled that bit of hacksaw blade through; he'd earned a favor from Tsezar that evening; he'd bought that tobacco. And he hadn't fallen ill. He'd go over it.*
>
> *A day without a dark cloud. Almost a happy day. There were three thousand six hundred and fifty-three days like that in his stretch, from the first clang of the rail to the last clang of the rail.*
>
> *Three thousand six hundred and fifty-three days. The three extra days were for leap years (158).*

Intercessions

That we may add beauty to feasts;

That we may not make heedless promises.

Prayer

> *God of Compassion,*
> * have mercy upon those of us*
> *who have never*
> * hungered,*
> *   nor thirsted,*
> *   nor been strangers,*
> *   nor naked,*
> *   nor ill,*
> *   nor in prison,*
> *   through Jesus Christ our Saviour. Amen*

328 Saturday of the Fourth Week of the Year

Heb 13:15-17; 1 Kgs 3:4-13; Mark 6:30-34

> *. . . But mercy is above this sceptered sway,*
> *It is enthroned in the hearts of kings,*
> *It is an attribute to God himself,*
> *And earthly power doth then show likest God's*
> *When mercy seasons justice. . . .*
> (Shakespeare, Merchant of Venice, 4.1.191–95)

> *Padre nuestro que estás en la tierra . . . .*
> *eres ese Viejo que da migas de pan a los pájaros del paseo.*
> (Gloria Fuertes, "Oración," Antología, Cano, 243)

The theme of shepherding dominates our readings. In the ancient world "shepherd" was a synonym for king or ruler. He was certainly not clothed in a long, white robe holding a woolly lamb, as Jesus is depicted so often in Christian art. No, the shepherd was an athletic figure of tremendous endurance, initiative and courage. He would "gird up his loins" to rescue sheep or goats (he might have a black and white flock) from wild animals or dangerous terrains; he was obliged to seek water and new pastures for them. He had to endure all the inclemencies of the weather.

As far back as Homer the shepherd was a model for the monarch. This poet calls the monarch "shepherd of the peoples." He is the preserver of the lives of his subjects (cf. Ezek 34). Similarly the philosopher, Seneca the Younger, wrote to the emperor, Nero, the following advice:

Yet of all men none is better graced by mercy than a king or prince.
For great power confers grace and glory only when it is potent for
benefit. . . . He alone has firm and well-grounded greatness whom
all men know to be as much their friend as he is their superior. . . .

(De Clementia 3:1)

Nero, notorious for his cruelty and arbitrary punishments and executions of pagans and Christians, had abundant need of this advice.

Intercessions

That God may give all leaders an understanding
heart to judge . . . and to distinguish right from wrong;

That we, like Jesus, may realize the need for rest.

Prayer

O God, your Son portrayed his ministry
as a shepherd's like David's.
May we develop the talents (charismata) of a shepherd,
an alacrity to lay down our lives for those in our care;
agility in performing deeds of loving kindness;
courage in the face of danger;
resourcefulness in barren situations
and knowledge and sensitivity
for each one under our care. Amen.

74 Fifth Sunday of the Year
Cycle A

Isa 58:7-10; 1 Cor 2:1-5; Matt 5:13-16

How far that little candle throws his beams!
So shines a good deed in a naughty world.

(Shakespeare, Merchant of Venice, 5.1.90–91)

¡Clara fuente de luz nuevo y hermoso,
rico de luminarias patrio cielo!
¡Casa de la verdad, sin sombra o velo . . . .

(Juan de la Cruz, Al Cielo)

The Isaiah reading explains that deeds of loving kindness and justice constitute real "fasting" in God's eyes and it is these which cause "light" to shine. In many religious cultures "light" is a symbol of godliness and supernatural wisdom and revelation. The Dead Sea Scrolls, for example, call the righteous the "Children of Light." God *per se* is often portrayed as light or wearing a garment of light. In Genesis 1 light was the first element created by God. Similarly the Word of God in Scripture is described as a lamp or light to guide people on the way of righteousness. So the first reading tells us that practices, like fasting, do not necessarily show that we have received God's revelation. However, deeds of loving kindness do because they portray the very essence of God and godliness. In the gospel lesson, Jesus tells his disciples that they can be the light of the world and the salt of the earth. The reason for this is that those who are close to Jesus share in his prerogative as Light of the World. Matthew may not have in mind light as a lamp but rather the light of the world which is the sun. The sun not only brings light but warmth and growth. It is the power which keeps all things alive. The sun was also the symbol of God's sovereignty which would appear in the last times. So Jesus tells his disciples to be the "Sun of the World." In like manner the disciples are the salt of the earth; they season and preserve life. Salt is almost the synonym for the essence of life-giving forces. The disciples, therefore, are to add "relish" to the gospel message. St. Francis of Assisi wrote a hymn to the Sun.

> Praise to thee, my Lord, for all thy creatures,
> Above all Brother Sun
> Who brings us the day and lends us his light.
>> (St. Francis of Assisi, *The Song of Brother Sun and of All His Creatures*)

Intercessions

> That we may understand the true nature of fasting;
>
> For those who add to the world's darkness and pain;
>
> For us that we may not rely on human eloquence but on the power of the Spirit.

Prayer

> True Sun of Justice
> you make your sun shine on the good and the wicked.

May we, your covenant partners,
  seek to shed the sunrays of kindness
upon friend and foe. Amen.

75 Fifth Sunday of the Year
Cycle B

Job 7:1-4, 6-7; 1 Cor 9:16-19, 22-23; Mark 1:29-39

Sleep that knits up the ravelled sleave of care,
The death of each day's life, sore labour's bath,
Balm of hurt minds, great nature's second course,
Chief nourisher in life's feast.

(Shakespeare, Macbeth, 2.2.36–39)

. . . y bien haya el que inventó el sueño, capa que cubre todos
los humanos pensamientos, manjar que quita la hambre, agua que
ahuyenta la sed, fuego que calienta el frío, frío que templa el ardor,
y, finalmente, moneda general con que todas las cosas se compran,
balanza y peso que iguala al pastor con el rey y al simple con el
discreto.

(Miguel de Cervantes, Don Quijote de la Mancha, II, 68)

The first reading records Job's despair and insomnia. In the gospel lesson, we find Jesus catching a time for prayer during the early hours of the morning but, even then, the crowds pursue him. Sleep was important in the ancient world. The Greek saw him as a god, the son of *Nyx* (Night), and the brother of *Thanatos* (Death). Although he belonged to the underworld he was seen as gentle and kind to humans. They thought of him as a winged youth who poured sleep-producing medicine from a horn or touched the weary with a branch. Sleep was regarded as holy because it was the medium of dreams which were seen as revelations from God. But in European culture sleep was also revered:

O magic sleep! O comfortable bird,
That broodeth ov'r the troubled sea of the mind
Till it is hushed and smooth!   (Keats, *Endymion*)

Now blessings light on him that first invented this same sleep!
It covers a man all over, thoughts and all, like a cloak; 'tis meat

for the hungry, drink for the thirsty, heat for the cold, and cold
for the hot. 'Tis the current coin that purchases all the pleasures
of the world cheap; and the balance that sets the king and the shep-
herd, the fool and the wise man even.

(Miguel deCervantes, Don Quixote de la Mancha)

Sleep is the image of death but awakening is also the image of the resurrection.

Intercessions

For those who suffer from insomnia;

For ministers that they may, like Paul, offer the gospel without
charge.

Prayer

God of Kindness, you give to your beloved ones sleep,
partitioning day from night,
resting body, mind and soul,
making possible a new beginning each day.
Make our nightly sleep
be a prelude
to our everlasting rest. Amen.

76 Fifth Sunday of the Year
Cycle C

Isa 6:1-2, 3-8; 1 Cor 15:1-11; Luke 5:1-11

Before I formed you in the womb I knew you,
before you were born I dedicated you,
a prophet to the nations I appointed you. . . .
See I place my words in your mouth!
This day I set you
over nations and over kingdoms.
To root up and to tear down,
to destroy and to demolish,
to build and to plant.

(Jer 1:5, 9-10)

El pan es dorado como una patena;
es copón de granos, de seno fecundo;
el pan es Sol santo que todo lo llena,
y su ara es la esfera redonda del mundo.

(Salvador Rueda, *El Pan, Antología*, Onis, 108)

The theme of the first and third reading is election and discipleship. Isaiah appears to have answered God's call through a mystical experience in the Temple. The disciples received theirs during the course of their working day (night). In both readings the one who is called professes unworthiness. In Isaiah an angel responds to this confession by cleansing the prophet's lip with a burning coal. It might interest readers to know that in some Eastern Christian churches the sacred host is called the "coal." This, together with the singing of the Holy, Holy, Holy (the Sanctus), placed the Eucharist in the context of the call of Isaiah. In the gospel lesson, Peter's profession of unworthiness is followed by Jesus' call to discipleship. The Pauline reading also mentions the theme of unworthiness and the apostle's mystical experience on the road to Damascus.

Intercessions

That we might not evade our mission
by a pretence of unworthiness;

That we might know what it is to be a
disciple of the resurrected Christ.

Prayer

O Almighty God, who hast knit together thine elect in one communion and fellowship, in the mystical body of thy Son Christ our Lord; Grant us grace so to follow thy blessed Saints in all virtuous and godly living, that we may come to those unspeakable joys, which thou hast prepared for them that unfeignedly love thee. Amen.   (*Book of Common Prayer*, 1662)

or,

Impartial caller of the wise and the simple,
of the graced and the graceless,
enable us to hear the whisper of your Spirit
over the noisy gong of the world
and the desires of our own hearts. Amen.

329   Monday of the Fifth Week of the Year

Gen 1:1-19; 1 Kgs 8:1-7, 9-13; Mark 6:53-56

To wake the soul by tender strokes of art,
To raise the genius, and to mend the heart;
To make mankind, in conscious virtue bold,
Live o'er each scene, and be what they behold:
For this the Tragic Muse first trod the stage.

(Pope, *Prologue to Mr. Addison's Cato*)

Creatures of a day, what is a man? What is he not? Mankind is
a dream of a shadow. But when a god-given brightness comes, a
radiant light rests on men, and a gentle life.

(Pindar, *Pythian Odes*)

. . . Aquí me tienes,
Señor, desnudo como el árbol. Dame
tu bautismo de lluvias y tu crisma
de sol, y dame vestiduras nuevas,
inmaculadas.

(Enrique Díez-Canedo, "Oración en el Jardín," *Antología*, Onis, 636)

Our lessons deal with creation, consecration and healing. The first
reading speaks of God as creator. In the Bible there are three stories
of creation. The earliest is Genesis 2:4b-25. Here God is portrayed dra-
matically, poetically, in anthropomorphic terms. God creates Adam
from clay and Eve from Adam's rib: the actual creation of the world
is summarized very concisely. The second account is in Genesis 1:1–
2:4a. Here there is an orderly method of creation and both man and
woman are created together: both are in the image and likeness of God.
The third description of creation is found in Sirach 17. It reads as
follows:

The Lord from the earth created man,
in his own image he made him.
Limited days of life he gives him
and makes him return to earth again.
He endows man with a strength of his own,
and with power over all things else on earth.
He put fear of him in all flesh,
and gives him rule over the beasts and birds.

He forms men's tongues and eyes and ears,
and imparts to them an understanding heart.
With wisdom and knowledge he fills them;
good and evil he shows them.
He looks with favour upon their hearts,
and shows them his glorious works.
That they may describe the wonders of his deeds
and praise his holy name.
He set before them knowledge,
a law of life as their inheritance:
An everlasting covenant he made with them,
his commandments he has revealed to them.
His majestic glory their eyes beheld,
his glorious voice their ears heard.
He says to them, "Avoid all evil";
each of them he gives precepts about his fellow men.
Their ways are ever known to him,
they cannot be hidden from his eyes. (Sir 17:1-13)

Skehan and di Lella comment[8] on humankind made in God's image. They say that it is "the charter statement of human dignity and equality for all men, women, and children in the sight of God" (282). In this poem, God's abundant gifts to humankind are listed. They are sensory, psychological, intellectual and moral (282). The reference to humankind hearing God's voice and seeing his glory alludes to the covenant on Mount Sinai (Exod 19:2–20:17 and Deut 5:1-22). The command to avoid evil appears to point to the negative commandments in the Decalogue (the Ten Commandments) and the precepts about one's neighbour to the second part of the Decalogue (282–283).

In the last two accounts of creation woman loses her inferior position. This should gladden the heart of both women and men. In the gospel lesson, Jesus is healer, that is, the restorer of humankind to their original perfection or even more.

Intercessions

That we may seek to maintain a harmony in nature;
That the glory of God may fill the temples of our souls.

[8]P. W. Skehan and A. A. Di Lella, *The Wisdom of Ben Sira* (Garden City, New York: Doubleday and Bantan, 1987).

Prayer

> God, Prodigal Creator of Humankind,
>   let us see your glory and hear your voice again,
> as it echoes through the heroic and compassionate voice
>   of Jesus Christ, your son, our brother. Amen.

330 Tuesday of the Fifth Week of the Year

Gen 1:20–2:4; 1 Kgs 8:22-23, 27-30; Mark 7:1-13

> *What is hateful to you, do not to your neighbour:*
> *that is the whole Torah; the rest is commentary. Go, study.*
>   (Rabbi Hillel)

> *Iglesia frutera*
> *sentada en una esquina de la vida . . . .*
>   (Jorge Carrera Andrade, "Domingo," *Antología*, Onis, 1162)

The first lesson speaks about the abundant creativity and bounty of God and how s/he deemed everything good. On the seventh day God rested from the divine labours as if to contemplate in peace the divine artistry. But the Gospel tells about over-scrupulous people who perform ritual cleansings as if creation were polluted. They also make some very restrictive laws which burden people, especially the poor, and which circumvent primary commandments, such as taking care of one's parents. How easily does religion become institutionalized, legislated, out of kilter with human needs and how often does this presuppose a rather stingy, hidebound God, not the God of liberality whom we find in the first lesson. The classical Hebrew prophets frequently denounced such religious practices. Indeed, they speak so sharply that sometimes one has the impression that they repudiate religious ceremonies altogether (e.g. Amos 4:4-5; Isa 1:10-16). The hedging around of God's word with multifarious rules and regulations spells not only a religion "gone wrong" but a poor image of God and also a deep sense of insecurity. We need to develop a kinder, perhaps even a more jocund, image of God.

Intercessions

> *That we might attain a correct balance between*
>   *piety and social conscience;*

That we might revel in the very
  good things of creation.

Prayer

God of Sincerity,
  you are offended by empty worship.
Let our hands which clap
  be used to give.
Let our voices which sing
  be used to comfort and encourage.
Let our feet which dance
  never tire in helping the weary.
Let us not multiply our words
  nor display our piety.
With due discretion let us
  "comfort the afflicted
    and afflict the comfortable." Amen.

331 Wednesday of the Fifth Week of the Year

Gen 2:5-9, 15-17; 1 Kgs 10:1-10; Mark 7:14-23

There is some soul of goodness in things evil,
Would men observingly distill it out.
(Shakespeare, Henry V, 4.1.4-5)

Hemos llegado a los bordes
de este mundo y la esperanza
ha huído quién sabe a dónde.
(Ángel Cruchaga Santa María, "Los Hijos de Job,"
Antología, Onis, 781)

Today's readings present us with an universal and well-nigh insoluble question, namely, the origin of evil. Genesis, using highly symbolic language, imputes it to the disobedience of humankind. Jesus sees evil arising from the human heart. Jewish tradition attributes human vacillation between good and evil to two impulses, the inclination to good (*yezer hà-tov*) and the inclination to evil (*yezer hà-ra*), that is, evil is regarded from a psychological and anthropological point of view. A person without God or moral guidance would give rein to the evil impulse (cf. Gen 8:21). This is not bad *per se* but is the untamed part of human nature. It leads to excess in sexual desire, anger, greed and other vices. In order to tame this tendency persons were encouraged to study and observe the Torah especially Scripture. In this way the good impulse was gradually developed. According to Jewish teaching it matures fully from the age of thirteen, that is, at the age of reason. This analogy is made in *Sukkah* 52a.

> R. Assi stated, The Evil Inclination is at first like the thread of
> a spider, but ultimately becomes like cart ropes, as it is said, Woe
> unto them that draw iniquity with cords of vanity, and sin as it
> were with a cart-rope.
> (Sukkah 52a)

R. Huna said:

> First it (the evil inclination) is called a passer-by, then he is called
> a guest, and finally he is called a man (that is, tenant of the house).
> (Sukkah 52)

There will be no evil impulse in the world to come.
  Carl Gustav Jung attributes evil not to God but to human beings.

> We need more understanding of human nature, because the only
> real danger that exists is man himself . . . We know nothing of
> man, far too little. His pysche should be studied because we are
> the origin of all coming evil.
> (BBC television interview)

Intercessions

> That we may be gentle and sensitive
>   towards the earth, our mother.

> That, like Solomon, we may seek
>   wisdom and understanding above all treasures.

Prayer

> God, Our Creator and Our Judge,
>   you placed the good and evil impulse in the human heart.
> Help us to create an atmosphere conducive to good;
>   to speak kind words,
>   to expel fear and invite love;
>   to challenge media which portray violence and sin
> and to foster that which is pure and beautiful. Amen.

332   Thursday of the Fifth Week of the Year

Gen 2:18-25; 1 Kgs 11:4-13; Mark 7:24-30

A woman of sense and manners is the finest and most delicate part
of God's creation, the glory of her Maker, and the great instance
of His singular regard to man.
(Daniel Defoe, An Essay Upon Projects)

¡Cuando así me acosan ansias andariegas
qué pena tan honda me da ser mujer!
(Juana de Ibarbourou, "Mujer," Once Grandes, 251)

The passage from Genesis has caused a great deal of controversy.
Some readers wish to see woman as inferior and subservient to man
but others emphasize the equality of the sexes. But it is important to
realize that in the ancient world there were as many goddesses as gods
and in the Jewish tradition the Spirit of God is always feminine. In
a similar way Wisdom is personified as woman (Prov 8; Sir 24; Wis
7). Further, in nonBiblical Jewish works the Spirit is called the
"Shekinah;" she is the immanance of God in the world, for
"Shekinah" means God's presence. She is a manifestation of God and
often described in terms of the radiant light. The Shekinah is said to
suffer, weep and go into exile for her people and similarly she also
rejoices when they are delivered from trouble. To some extent the
Shekinah is a mother figure.

Israel will be redeemed only when it forms one single band: when
all are united, they will receive the presence of the Shechinah.
Therefore Hillel said (Aboth 2.5), "Separate not thyself from the
community."   (*Tanhuma*, cf. *Berakhot* 496)

Intercessions

That we may possess that sense of
humour which scintillated between
Jesus and Syro-Phoenician woman;

That husbands and wives may be at peace
over their religious convictions.

Prayer

Creator of both Man and Woman,
help the world to see your image and likeness
in womankind.

Forgive your church for hindering her service,
  forgive the world for abusing her
in film, advertisement and pornography.
  May woman herself reverence
her body, mind and soul. Amen.

333 Friday of the Fifth Week of the Year

Gen 3:1-8; 1 Kgs 11:29-32; 12:19; Mark 7:31-37

O happy fault, which has deserved to have such and so mighty
a Redeemer.   (*Exsultet* on Holy Saturday)

. . . La tristeza
sacude, empero, que ella es el estrago
más corruptor de nuestras pobres vidas,
pues no es vivir vivir bajo su amago.
        (Miguel de Unamuno, "Redención," *Antología,* Onis, 220)

In the first and third reading we have a vivid contrast. In the myth from Genesis the woman sees the fruit and its attractiveness and after Adam and Eve had eaten it, their eyes were opened to their nakedness. This myth has assumed a disproportionate importance in Christian tradition although in Jewish tradition it was not really regarded as the "original sin." Jewish tradition emphasized more Genesis 6, the myth of the unnatural union between angels and women. It is better to see the eating of the forbidden tree as one of many "original sins" (in the plural), a few of which are related in Genesis 1-11, that is, the first murder by Cain (Gen 4); unnatural intercourse (Gen 6); drunkedness and/or dishonouring one's parent (Gen 9) and trying to attain to God through human means in the Tower of Babel (Gen 11). All these are basic, common ways in which people stray from God and from each other. In Genesis 3 the man and the woman try to go beyond their finiteness and humanity; they wish to become masters and mistresses of their own lives, perhaps even to become independent of God. In the gospel reading, we hear the deaf-mute whom Jesus cured. The healed man spoke plainly so that all wondered. In a way this lesson forms a complementary reading to Genesis. Speech distinguished human beings from animals; it was God's special gift to humankind but it was also mythologically the source of sin in the Genesis story where even the serpent speaks!

[On extra-terrestials in space exploration:] It is interesting to won-
der how things would go if they met an unfallen race. At first,
to be sure, they'd have a grand time jeering at, duping, and ex-
ploiting its innocence; but I doubt if our half-animal cunning would
long be a match for godlike wisdom, selfless valour, and perfect
unanimity.

(C. S. Lewis, *The World's Last Night and Other Essays*)

Intercessions

For the ability to refrain from judgment;

For the deaf that they may share with us
the gift of nonverbal communication.

Prayer

Author of All Compassion,
your Son taught us to forgive seventy times seven.
Grant us the grace
to see within ourselves
the image and likeness of God
and to forgive ourselves
seventy times seven. Amen.

334 Saturday of the Fifth Week of the Year

Gen 3:9-24; 1 Kgs 12:26-32; 13:33-34; Mark 8:1-10

Two of far nobler shape erect and tall,
Godlike erect, with native honor clad
In naked majesty seemed lords of all.   (Milton, *Paradise Lost*)

And of Milton himself, Wordsworth wrote,

Thy soul was like a star, and dwelt apart;
Thou hast a voice whose sound was like the sea:
Pure as the naked heavens, majestic, free,
So did thou travel on life's common way,
In cheerful godliness.   (Wordsworth, *London*)

Y extasiada murmuro:
—Cuerpo mío: ¡estás hecho
de sustancia inmortal!
(Juana de Ibarbourou, "Carne Inmortal," *Once Grandes*, 250)

To the Greek the naked body was the epitome of beauty. Vitruvius, an early Roman architect, speaks about making the temples of the gods in proportion and symmetry to the male body and the temples of female deities in proportion to the female body (Vitruvius, *Architecture*). He says that the Doric column has the "proportion of a man's body, its strength and grace," but in the temple built in honor of Diana the architects changed it to "feminine slenderness with the same measurement of feet," at the capital "they put volutes, like graceful curling hair, hanging over right and left. And arranging cymatia and festoons in place of hair, they ornamented the front, and over all the trunk (i.e. the shaft) they let fluing fall, like the folds of matronly robes; thus they proceeded to the invention of columns in two manners; one, manlike in appearance, bare, unadorned; the other feminine." They also designed a third kind of column, the Corinthian, that "imitates the slight figure of a maiden; because girls are represented with slighter dimensions because of their tender age, and admit of more graceful effects in ornament." Jewish and Christian traditions are more cautious about praising the body although it is always seen as the epitome of God's creation. With regard to the sin of Adam and Eve the rabbis speak about God's sorrow in imposing the punishment of death on Adam and his sorrow over human wickedness. They say that God pronounced sentence of Adam but released him on the Sabbath, talked to him and hoped that he would repent for God "made the attribute of mercy take precedence over the attribute of judgment" (Montefiore and Loewe, 236–237). All the divine pleasure is in beholding the lives of the righteous.

Intercessions

That we may multiply "loaves and fish"
for the poor of the world;

That we may not be like Jeroboam multiplying
idolatry but rather destroy our idols of
consumerism and indifferent individualism.

Prayer

God, Artist and Creator,
you have sculptured the human body with supreme grace

as temples of your Holy Spirit.
May we never mar this beauty. Amen.

77   Sixth Sunday of the Year
Cycle A

Sir 15:15-20; 1 Cor 2:6-10; Matt 5:17-37 or 5:20-22, 27-28, 33-34, 37

I see on an immense scale, and as clearly as in a demonstration
in a laboratory, that good comes out of evil; that the impartiality
of the Nature Providence is best; that we are made strong by what
we overcome; that man is man because he is as free to do evil as
to do good; that life is as free to develop hostile forms as to develop
friendly; that power waits upon him who earns it; that disease,
wars, the unloosened, devastating elemental forces have each and
all played their part in developing and hardening man and giving
him the heroic fiber.
(John Burroughs, Accepting the Universe)

Rogamos por vosotros y aprendemos
lo que cuesta la paz bien merecida.
(Enrique Badosa, "Balada para La Paz de los soldados,"
Los Derechos, 169)

Our first lesson addresses the subject of freewill and human responsibility which it lays upon us. No person can blame God for sin. God
sets before a person the choice of two ways, fire (death) or water (life).
The doctrine of the two ways is found in Scripture, e.g. Deuteronomy
30:15 where the choice is between life and prosperity, or death and
doom. Deuteronomy 28 includes the way of life: victory, prosperity,
fertility of field and family; and the way of death: defeat, sickness,
despoilment, exile, fruitless labour, invasion, siege, plagues. This doctrine is also found in the Dead Sea Scrolls; the covenanters choose
either the way of darkness or the way of light. The fruits of light include, "healing, great peace in a long life, and fruitfulness, together
with every everlasting blessing and eternal joy in life without end, a
crown of glory and a garment of majesty in unending light." (trans.
Vermès). The "way" is also used in the early Christian work called
the *Didache* or *The Teaching of the Apostles*. In the gospel lesson, Jesus

asks us to go beyond the literal interpretation of the Torah (the Decalogue). We are called to an even greater commitment.

Intercessions

That we may avoid all abusive, slovenly
and injurious language;

That we might seek that higher
wisdom which comes directly from God.

Prayer

God our Maker,
you endowed men and women
with the awesome power of freewill.
Clothe us with your wisdom
that by our choices we may contribute
to life and not death. Amen.

78 Sixth Sunday of the Year
Cycle B

Lev 13:1-2, 44-46; 1 Cor 10:31–11:1; Mark 1:40-45

Sleeping within mine orchard,
My custom always in the afternoon,
Upon my secure hour thy uncle stole,
With juice of cursed hebenon in a vial,
And in the porches of mine ears did pour
The leperous distilment; whose effect
Holds such enmity with blood of man,
That, swift as quicksilver, it courses through
The natural gates and alleys of the body;
And, with sudden vigour, it doth posset
And curd, like eager droppings into milk,
The thin and wholesome blood: so did it mine;
And a most instant tetter bark'd about,
Most lazar-like, with vile and loathsome crust,
All my smooth body.   (Shakespeare, *Hamlet*, 1.5.59–73)

Violentamente
tu olor se abrió como un abanico de miserias;
tu temblor se exhalaba
en un sahumario azul de podredumbre . . . .
                    (Clara Silva, "Lazaro, Donde Estabas? . . . ",
                                        Once Grandes, 339)

The present writer has visited two leper colonies. It was a most fruitful experience. In one sanatorium all the patients were preparing with great joy for the feast of Corpus Christi: the chaplain spoke about the intrinsic goodness and nobility of his congregation. In the other sanatorium, because our group could not speak the language of the patients, we showed our pleasure by shaking hands with each one. This simple gesture filled the lepers with happiness until many of them (those who were not too handicapped) began to sing, dance and play musical instruments. It was an unforgettable sight.

But the quotation from Shakespeare above might give us another inkling into the symbolism of "leprosy." The ghost, Hamlet's father, is describing how Hamlet's uncle poured poison into his ears and his body became like a leper. He died instantly. We might meditate on this. Have we poured the "leperous distilment" of gossip into people's ears until a third party appears as loathsome as a leper's body and they are shunned by other people and succumb to societal death? It is an arresting thought.

Intercessions

For lepers and AIDS (SIDA) victims;

For liberation theologians.

Prayer

God, you are clothed in the lucid robe of truth.
  Keep us, your friends, from every venomous word
and transform us into healers of those
  made leperous by our society. Amen.

79 Sixth Sunday of the Year
Cycle C

Jer 17:5-8; 1 Cor 15:12, 16-20; Luke 6:17, 20-26

To live content with small means; to seek elegance rather than lux-
ury, and refinement rather than fashion; to be worthy, not respect-
able, and wealthy, not rich; to study hard, think quietly, talk
gently, act frankly; to listen to stars and birds, to babes and sages,
with open heart; to bear all cheerfully, do all bravely, await occa-
sions, hurry never. In a word, to let the spiritual, unbidden and
unconscious, grow up through the common. This is to be my sym-
phony.   (W. H. Channing, *My Symphony*)

El pan es luz cautiva y apretada . . . .
      (Luis López Anglada, "El Pan de Todos," *Los Derechos*, 468)

Jeremiah delivered his prophetic message in a situation of extreme
conflict. He was a man of God who had to confront his own people
with their complacent theology and politics. He experienced ignomini-
ous suffering from them, even imprisonment and death threats. The
Lucan Jesus addresses a crowd of oppressed persons, oppressed economically and politically. It must have been grievous for the Palestinian farmer and his/her family to see rich Greco-Romans reaping
tremendous profits from their large estates "stolen" from the promised
land which God had meant to be equally divided among the tribes of
Israel. Both Jeremiah and Jesus exhort us to depend upon God and,
in a way, the Lucan Jesus promises the people a future utopia. Matthew 5:3-11 has spiritualized these beatitudes and omitted the woes.
But Luke confronts the situation. It is understandable that his Gospel
is loved so much by the theologians of liberation.
    A hundred years ago Carnegie said:

The problem of our age is the proper administration of wealth, so
that the ties of brotherhood may still bind together the rich and
poor in harmonious relationship.
                              (Andrew Carnegie, *Wealth*. From the
                              North American Review, June, 1889)

Intercessions

For those oppressed, deprived and violated;
For contentment.

Prayer

> *Covenant God,*
> *you did divide the land of Israel equably*
> *according to the number of persons in each tribe.*
> *Grant to our greedy and ambitious world*
> *the wisdom and charity*
> *to seek for a just distribution of land.*
> *Let us appreciate the sacred nature*
> *of territorial boundaries. Amen.*

335 Monday of the Sixth Week of the Year

Gen 4:1-15, 25; Jas 1:1-11; Mark 8:11-13

> *Confusion now hath made his masterpiece!*
> *Most sacrilegious murder hath broke ope*
> *The Lord's anointed temple, and stole thence*
> *The life o' the building.*   (Shakespeare, *Macbeth,* 2.3.72–75)

> *Y a ti, Caín, el sordo horror te apalpa,*
> *y huyes de nuevo, huyes.*
>   (Dámaso Alonso, "El Ultimo Cain," *Los Derechos,* 79)

Our Old Testament reading contains the story of the "original murder." For the believer, murder is devastating because it is the destruction of some one made in the image and likeness of God. In a certain way, it is blasphemy. But many criminals may kill because, seeing no value in their own lives, they assume there is no worth in another's life. In a Jewish text we read:

> *A man came to Raba and said, "The prefect of my town has ordered me to kill so and so, or he will kill me." Raba replied, "Let him kill you; do you commit no murder. Why should you think that your blood is redder than his? Perhaps his is redder than yours."*   (Pesahim 25b)

In another Rabbinic text we find:

> *Great is peace, for it the beings above, among whom is no jealousy or hate or contention or wrangling or quarrel or strife or envy,*

need peace, as it is said, "He creates peace in his high places"
(Job 25:2), how much more do the beings below, with whom all
these bad qualities are present, need peace. . . .

(Leviticus Rabbah 9:9)

Intercessions

That the epidemic of murder in our land be assuaged;

That we may see God's image in others.

Prayer

Triune God, you live in a relationship of loving friendship
between Father (Mother), Son and Holy Spirit.
Make us a mirror of your godhood
and turn us from our brutal ways. Amen.

336 Tuesday of the Sixth Week of the Year

Gen 6:5-8; 7:1-5, 10; Jas 1:12-18; Mark 8: 14-21

There is a tide in the affairs of men
Which, taken at the flood, leads on to fortune;
Omitted, all the voyage of their life
Is bound in shallows and in miseries.
On such a full sea are we now afloat,
And we must take the current when it serves,
Or lose our ventures.   (Shakespeare, *Julius Caesar*, 4.3.218–24)

Pero la vida, ahora mismo,
se precipita loca en cada grano de polvo . . . .
—¿Es que vuelve, decidme, el gran Diluvio?

(Isaac Felipe Azofeifa, "Poema de la Bomba H 1.
De Nuevo el diluvio," *Los Derechos*, 151)

A story of the flood (deluge) is found in most cultures. In a parallel
Babylonian text, the *Gilgamesh Epic*, the deities tell Utnapishtim to build
a boat and also to save every species of animal (respecting endangered
species!), his family and the skilled craftpersons. After the flood the
god blesses Utnapishtim and his wife with immortality. But the Hebrew God does not give immortality to Noah and his family. Rather

the writer empathizes the corruption of the earth. God saw evil in humankind and his/her heart was grieved. God feels emotion like a human being. S/he sees man and woman, who were the crown of his/her creation, polluting more and more the beautiful earth that s/he had made. So s/he, as it were, washes it away and gives everything a fresh start, a new beginning with the past no longer hanging over one. The description of the flood is powerful. The author shows the cosmic waters from heaven and the fountains below the earth meeting together to overwhelm the earth and set the stage for a "new creation." The text should speak clearly to us today. We are polluting the earth day by day with our trash, our chemicals, our wars, our waste. In contrast to many cultures, including the Hebrew, earth was seen as a mother, and murder and grave sins polluted her. The earth receives our abuse in silence. As Walt Whitman writes:

> *The earth does not argue,*
> *Is not pathetic, has no arrangements,*
> *Does not scream, haste, persuade, threaten, promise,*
> *Makes no discriminations, has no conceivable failures,*
> *Closes nothing, refuses nothing, shuts none out.*
>
> (Walt Whitman, *To the Saver of Words*)

Intercessions

That we may relate to the earth as a living being;

That we may treasure her resources.

Prayer

O God, Creator of our Prodigal Earth,
  We have raped, disembowelled, burnt and bled her.
Forgive us, her heartless children.
  Teach us to learn
from the patient endurance of her martyrdom.
Amen.

337 Wednesday of the Sixth Week of the Year

Gen 8:6-13, 20-22; Jas 1:19-27; Mark 8:22-26

There is triple sight in blindness keen. (Keats, *To Homer*)

Aquesta me guiaba
más cierto que la luz de mediodía,
adonde me esperaba,
quien yo bien me sabía,
en parte donde nadie parecía.
(Juan de la Cruz, "Cancion de la subida del Monte Carmelo")

Mark includes two stories about the healing of blindness in his gospel. They both stand in strategical positions. The one described in today's reading stands before Peter's great confession of Jesus' messianic status and it shows a gradual clearing of vision. It symbolizes the growing faith and spiritual understanding of the "little" people, not only the disciples. In Mark the "little" people often have more faith than the disciples. The second account is found in Mark 10:46-52 after the confession, the transfiguration and Jesus' prediction of his own suffering and the true nature of discipleship, which involves suffering and misunderstanding. It shows a person immediately healed from his blindness. It denotes the full understanding of Jesus' nature and mission. This understanding is only possible when one comprehends the necessity of Jesus' humiliation and death, which characterize his generosity and selflessness. His comportment was very different from the ways of many earthly persons. Real blindness is apathy, ignorance, inability to look beyond oneself and employ one's days in service to others. Wilder expresses this quite well.

That's what it was to be alive. To move about in a cloud of ignorance; to go up and down trampling on the feelings of those about you. To spend and waste time as though you had a million years. To be always at the mercy of one self-centered passion, or another. Now you know—that's the happy existence you wanted to go back to. Ignorance and blindness. (T. N. Wilder, *Our Town*)

Further, Picasso, one of the most celebrated artists of our time, says of his profession:

Painting is a blind man's profession. He paints not what he sees,
but what he feels, what he tells himself about what he has seen.

(Picasso, *Childhood*)

Intercessions

That we may be able to acknowledge our blindness;

That we may use our fleeting days with wisdom.

Prayer

God of Blind Justice,
  the soldiers blindfolded and mocked
the "light of the world"—
  yet his sight was not dimmed or extinguished.
Deliver us from that arrogance
  which claims insight into the impenetrable. Amen.

338   Thursday of the Sixth Week of the Year

Gen 9:1-13; Jas 2:1-9; Mark 8:27-33

Will all great Neptune's ocean wash this blood
Clean from my hand? No, this my hand will rather
The multitudinous seas incarnadine.

(Shakespeare, *Macbeth*, 2.2.59–61)

Alma, buscarte has en Mí,
Ya a Mí buscarme has en ti.   (Teresa de Jesús, *Poesía*)

Murder is defacing the image and likeness of God. It is always atrocious because it deprives man or woman of their most precious possession, Life, with all its opportunities for enrichment, for service, for sheer joy in living, and for the building of community. No one really realizes the magnitude of this gift except the man or woman who has come near to death or, for some reason—being a hostage, being imprisoned, being severely handicapped—knows what it is to be deprived of the fullness of life. Yet we take life so much for granted and we live in a society where a large percentage of people underestimate their own lives and consequently take lightly the deprivation of another's life and the part this life plays in the community. In the gospel, we see how Jesus understood that his enemies would destroy the Author of Life and try to negate the gift of the incarnation to humankind.

Affirmation of life is the spiritual act by which man ceases to live unreflectively and begins to devote himself to his life with reverence in order to raise it to its true value. To affirm life is to deepen, to make more inward, and to exalt the will to live.
(Albert Schweitzer, *Out of My Life and Thought*)

Intercessions

For the unborn dead;

For the ability to celebrate life.

Prayer

Life of the World, Author of All Being,
 purge our contempt for life.
In the mirror of our transient life
 teach us to see the reflection of your image and likeness
in every creature.
 May we travel with curiosity and joy
to the reality of eternity. Amen.

339 Friday of the Sixth Week of the Year

Gen 11:1-9; Jas 2:14-24, 26; Mark 8:34–9:1

They say that our madness consists in the fact that we put a crucified man in second place after the unchangeable and eternal God, the creator of the world. (Justin Martyr, *Apologia* 1.13)

Vénganle desamparos,
Cruces, desgracias;
Siendo Dios su tesoro,
Nada le falta.

(Teresa de Jesús, "Nada te Turbe")

In the gospel reading today, Jesus speaks about the disciple's duty to take up the cross and follow him. Of paramount importance is the phrase "any one who is *ashamed* of me or my doctrine . . ." Honor and shame were pivotal values in the ancient world and the most shameful, degrading and jested death was execution on the cross. In this gospel lesson, therefore, Jesus is challenging his disciples to adopt an entirely new way of life, where some things which are shameful will become honorable and some which are honorable will be shameful. Crucifixion has a very long and painful history and in the time of Jesus it did not abate. Crucifixions and impalements were implemented in the thousands. Josephus, the Jewish historian, says that in the Roman/Jewish war, 66–74 A.D., Titus crucified five hundred people a day before the walls of Jerusalem hoping that the city would capitulate. With this background it is understandable that the Greco-Roman world was profoundly shocked when Christians claimed that their leader and sovereign was a crucified man risen from the dead. For example, Minucius Felix places such words as the following in the mouth of Caecilius, a pagan who in debating with Christian, sees the Christian faith as a "sick delusion," "senseless and crazy superstition," which leads to the annihilation of genuine religion (Hengel, *Crucifixion*). Some believed that the crucified person was so utterly destroyed that s/he could have no afterlife. Yet the Christians claimed that Jesus rose from the dead. Jesus' admonition is not addressed solely to men, for women, too, could be crucified or impaled.

Intercessions

For an understanding of Jesus' death;

For all innocent persons condemned
to imprisonment, torture and death.

Prayer

God of Acute Sensitivity and Tender Compassion
heal the savagery of our human nature.
Where we have torn
let your gentle fingers knit together;
where we have shamed,
share your honour with our victims;
where we have spread fear,
coax with the tenderness of your love.
Where we have dealt a lethal blow
let the power of Christ's resurrection shine forth. Amen.

340 Saturday of the Sixth Week of the Year

Heb 11:1-7; Jas 3:1-10; Mark 9:2-13

While with an eye made quiet by the power
Of harmony, and the deep power of joy,
We see into the life of things. (Wordsworth, *Tintern Abbey*)

Un árbol me brindaba su paz . . . A la ventura,
pasé cabe la sombra sin probar su frescura.
(Enrique González, "El Retorno Imposible,"
Antología, Onis 501)

The reading from Hebrews and the Gospel of Mark fit closely together. Hebrews speaks about faith in the midst of trials and acute suffering. It is not the faith of people who wait anxiously for miracles and "cures" but of those who have understood what it is to suffer for truth and love and for the God whom they trust and love. In the gospel lesson, Jesus allows his disciples a glimpse of his future glory through the transfiguration and immediately after that he begins to teach them clearly about his suffering, rejection and resurrection. Suffering is only endurable when there is a goal. In Hebrews 12:1-2 (the climax of our reading today) the author exhorts his readers:

. . . let us keep our eyes fixed on Jesus, who inspires and perfects
our faith. For the sake of the joy which lay before him he endured
the cross, heedless of its shame. (Heb 12:2)

Our goal is the glorified Jesus. And reflecting both upon Jesus' suffering and the suffering of other friends, who have inspired us by their heroic stature during grief, we may say with Odysseus:

But we two (Eumaeus, the swineherd, and Odysseus) will drink
and feast in the hut, and will take delight each in the other's griev-
ous woes, as we recall them to mind. For in after time a man finds
joy even in woes, whosoever has suffered much, and wandered
much. (Homer, *Odyssey*)

Intercessions

For the transfiguration of our world;
For the ability to share grief and joy.

Prayer

Mysterious God, you walk among us
  both in grief and in felicity.

Teach us the secret
  of life enshrined in death,
of joy buried in the fertile earth of pain. Amen.

80 Seventh Sunday of the Year
Cycle A

Lev 19:1-2, 17-18; 1 Cor 3:16-23; Matt 5:38-48

Still in thy right hand carry gentle peace.
(Shakespeare, Henry VIII, 3.2.444)

Sólo veía sangre derramada.
(Dámaso Alonso, "Palinodia: La Sangre,"
Los Derechos, 107)

The first reading speaks about the sacrosanctity of members of the covenant community: they are to be brothers and sisters and, therefore, should never be injured in thought, word or deed. For the Hebrew, any violence within the brotherhood was sacrilegious, moral turpitude to the highest degree. Jesus takes this teaching a stage further and forbids retaliation, whether because of bodily injury or insult, or litigation or compulsory "military service" (helping to carry the baggage of the occupying army or forced loan of your draft animals). All this called for a reasonable, controlled approach to the "enemy," an approach without anger. Perhaps my readers might find helpful the following quotations from Seneca's treatise on anger.

> *What is more hostile than anger? Man is born for mutual help; anger for mutual destruction . . . Anger . . . is bent on punishment, and that such a desire should find a harbour in man's most peaceful breast accords least of all with his nature. For human life is founded on kindness and concord, and is bound into an alliance for common help, not by terror, but by mutual love.*
> (Seneca, On Anger)

And again:

> *Anger aims at nothing splendid or beautiful . . . it seems to me*
> *to show a feeble and harassed spirit, one conscious of its own weak-*
> *ness and oversensitive, just as the body is when it is sick and co-*
> *vered with sores and makes moan at the slightest touch.*
>
> (Seneca, *On Anger*)

Intercessions

> *For the healing of litigious society in America;*
> *For the sacrosanctity of church members.*

Prayer

> God of Domestic Peace,
>   we live in a time when domestic violence
> robs many of life and love.
>   We place under your tender protection
> all families prone to abuse and violence. Amen.

81 Seventh Sunday of the Year
Cycle B

Isa 43:18-19, 21-22, 24-25; 2 Cor 1:18-22; Mark 2:1-12

> *To be a Christian means to forgive the inexcusable, because God*
> *has forgiven the inexcusable in you.*
>
> (C. S. Lewis, *The Weight of Glory*)

> *Tú eres el agua obscura*
> *que mana por adentro de la roca . . . .*
>
> (Dulce María Loynaz, "Agua Escondida,"
> *Once Grandes*, 423)

The dominant theme of our first two readings is forgiveness. In the first lesson God tells the people through the prophet, Isaiah, that he will blot out of his memory all the sins which they committed and for which they were sent as exiles into Babylon. God's forgiveness comprises not only the forgetting of past infidelity but the creating of something new, a transformation. This is symbolized by water appearing in the desert; that is, he creates a life force in the barren places. In a similar way in the gospel lesson, Jesus forgives the sins of the paralytic but he also transforms him in soul and body so that all his spiritual and physical powers are restored, reinvigorated. This message makes us pause. We ask for forgiveness and forgetting of past wrongs, do we also seek for transformation?

> They say best men are molded out of faults,
> And, for the most, become much more the better
> For being a little bad.
> (Shakespeare, Measure for Measure 5.1.440–42)

Intercessions

> That forgiveness may awake new life within us;
>
> That we may never lose the hope of conversion.

Prayer

> Redeemer God,
>   you brought from your treasures
>   incalculable wealth
>   through the sin of Adam and Eve.
> Throw the mantle of your transforming Spirit
>   over every social sin. Amen.

82 Seventh Sunday of the Year
Cycle C

1 Sam 26:2, 7-9, 12-13, 22-23; 1 Cor 15:45-49; Mark 6:27-38

> Only the brave know how to forgive . . .
> A coward never forgave; it is not in his nature.
> (L. Sterne, Sermons)

> Señor, para mi amor al arte, perdón.
> (Fernández Morene, "Oración")

In the action of David in the first lesson we have an outstanding example of the teaching which Jesus would give later, namely, not only the forgiveness of one's enemy but deeds of loving kindness towards him/her. Saul was persecuting David out of jealousy and intended to kill him but David regarded the person of the king as sacrosanct. A monarch was chosen by God and anointed before the people and, therefore, to injure or kill him was a sin before God and a danger to oneself and the people. Jesus was not the first person to teach nonviolence. For example, about thirty years before he was born there lived a rabbi called Hillel, he was of the school of the Pharisees but was flexible and peaceloving. It might be helpful to read some of his sayings:

> He (the man who wished to convert to Judaism) went to Hillel
> and Hillel said to him:
> What is hateful to you, do not do to your neighbour:
> that is the whole Torah (God's revelation); the rest is com-
> mentary; go, study.
> (N. N. Glatzer, Hillel the Elder [New York:
Schocken Books, 1966] 74)

> Ye see, my children, what great things I endured that I should
> not put my brethren to shame. Do ye also, love one another, and
> with long-suffering hide ye one another's faults. For God delight-
> eth in the unity of brethren, and in the purpose of a heart that
> takes pleasure in love.   (Glatzer, 75)

Before the time of Hillel, another pious Jew, during a battle between two relatives, said the following prayer:

> O God, the king of the whole world!
> Since those who stand now with me are Thy people
> and those that are besieged are also Thy priests,
> I pray
> that Thou mayest not listen to the prayers of those against these,
> nor bring to effect what these pray against those. (Glatzer, 65)

Intercessions

> That we might grieve over sin;
>
> That we may hide the faults of others.

Prayer

> All-Merciful One,
>   you have taught us to forgive
> seventy times seven.

Relieve us
from the tyranny of brutish silence;
from forgiveness of the lips and not the heart;
from cankerous harping on faults or apologies;
from crafty devices for vengeance and manipulation
and from body language
which murders
our words of forgiveness,
through Christ, Our Lord. Amen.

341 Monday of the Seventh Week of the Year

Sir 1:1-10; Jas 3:13-18; Mark 9:14-29

He who learns must suffer. And even in our sleep pain that can-
not forget falls drop by drop upon the heart, and in our own de-
spair, against our will, comes wisdom to us by the awful grace
of God. (Aeschylus, *Agamemnon*)

¡Padre, empléame estas manos,
que se me hacen sanguinarias!
(Eduardo Marquina, "Ganarás El Pan," *Los Derechos,* 344)

Wisdom in antiquity usually meant a quality rather than an activity. It denoted a special kind of knowledge. A wise person was one who possessed mastery and experience in his/her area of competence, e.g. statesman or builder. Wisdom was a gift of God which descended from heaven to humankind. She was closely associated with "goodness" and resulted from the possession and practice of the four cardinal virtues of prudence, fortitude, justice and temperance. The wise person was one who perceived the reality of the world around him/her, was able to penetrate the human mind and who gave sound advice and discernment on a natural and supernatural level. Wisdom combined theory and practice. In the Hebrew Scriptures it meant an informed, competent action which was able to deal intelligently with the problems and vicissitudes of life and bring them into harmony.

We see these principles in our three lessons. In the first we are told that all wisdom comes from God and that God *per se* because God is Wisdom. In the second reading from James wisdom is closely associated with ethics and a consciousness of the needs of the community especially with regard to justice (one of the four cardinal virtues). In the gospel reading, Jesus is shown as the wise and compassionate person who knows how to bring harmony to the distraught mind of a child. The healing is closely associated with the faith and humility of the father but it is also highly symbolic.

Intercessions

For a perception of wisdom in the unlettered;

For an appreciation of feminine wisdom.

Prayer

O Wondrous God,
*   you have penetrated humankind*
with the glory of your wisdom.
*   Teach us to dismantle*
ourselves of all darkness and to robe
*   ourselves with your light. Amen.*

342 Tuesday of the Seventh Week of the Year

Sir 2:1-11; Jas 4:1-10; Mark 9:30-37

The little world of childhood with its familiar surroundings is a model of the greater world. The more intensively the family has stamped its character upon the child, the more it will tend to feel and see its earlier miniature world again in the bigger world of adult life. Naturally this is not a conscious, intellectual process.
(C. G. Jung, The Theory of Psychoanalysis)

Es verdad, no es un cuento;
hay un Angel Guardián
que te toma y te lleva como el viento
y con los niños va por donde van.
(Gabriela Mistral, "El Angel Guardián," Desolación, 96)

The first and the third lesson fit snugly together. In the Sirach reading the writer describes the situation of the *anawin,* the poor, faithful ones of God who meekly endure tribulation with all their trust placed in God. They know that eventually God will save them. In the gospel reading, Jesus anticipates this role for himself. People will be envious, provoked, confronted by him and they will sentence him to summary arrest, torture and a cruel, shameful death, which was usually reserved for those of the servile class, slaves. Yet his hope will be in God who will raise him from the dead. In explaining this to his disciples he takes a child. We do not know whether this was a little girl or a little boy because the Greek text uses the neuter for the noun and pronouns. Little children usually lack ambition, avarice and arrogance. Psalm 131 expresses similar sentiments:

> O Lord, my heart is not proud,
>   nor are my eyes haughty;
> I busy not myself with great things,
>   nor with things too sublime for me.
> Nay rather, I have stilled and quieted
>   my soul like a weaned child.
> Like a weaned child on its mother's lap.
>   [so is my soul within me]
> O Israel, hope in the Lord,
>   both now and for evermore.

Kahlil Gibran also has some arresting words on children:

> You may give them your love but not your thoughts,
>   For they have their own thoughts.
> You may house their bodies but not their souls,
>   For their souls dwell in the house of tomorrow,
>   which you cannot visit, not even in your dreams.
> You may strive to be like them, but seek not to make them like you,
>   For life goes not backward nor tarries with yesterday.
> You are the bows from which your children
>   as living arrows are sent forth.   (On Children)

Intercessions

> For children who lack love;
>
> For a return to the excitement of childhood discovery.

Prayer

> O, God, you elected the shepherd boy, David,
>   in preference to his brothers.
> Enable us to look, not at outward appearance,
>   but into the heart.
> May we neither despise nor overlook
>   those of humble origins or less privileged situation. Amen.

343 Wednesday of the Seventh Week of the Year

Sir 4:11-19; Jas 4:13-17; Mark 9:38-40

Well, let's go on disagreeing but don't let us judge. What doesn't
suit us may suit possible converts of a different type . . . "Mind
one's own business" is a good rule in religion as in other things.
(C. S. Lewis, *Letters*, March 13, 1956)

Tu belleza se llamará también misericordia, y consolará el corazón
de los hombres. (Gabriela Mistral, *Decálogo del Artista*)

In essence our readings pertain to discipleship, whether "formal"
or "informal." The first lesson speaks about Wisdom as a Woman
Teacher, one of considerable discipline, even though she may deal
tenderly with her students. Her disciples are described as those

> *who seek her;*
> *who love her;*
> *who hold her fast;*
> *who serve her;*
> *who obey her;*
> *who hearken to her;*
> *who trust her.*

These are all marks of discipleship. Their reward is fullness of life for
those who serve Wisdom and serve God, and those who love her, God
loves. Those who reject her, fail to acquire the true meaning of life.
In the gospel, Jesus advises John not to prevent the work of an exorcist, even though he is not a disciple. I think that Jesus may see in
this exorcist the beginnings of faith and discipleship. He has obviously
"hearkened" to Jesus or those who reported to him about Jesus; he
trusts in Jesus's name and its power and, in his own way, he is "seeking" Jesus. Further, he is serving others by delivering them from af-
fliction. Jesus' message is one of tolerance, of encouragement and of
trusting divine providence and wisdom to work in the heart of the un-
believer. He rejects the exclusive attitude of John. Given time Wisdom
may, indeed, "reveal her secrets" to the strange exorcist.

Intercessions

That we might respect the beliefs of others;
That we might draw near to Lady Wisdom.

Prayer

Meticulous Architect of this Resplendent Universe,
you wove her multicolored fabric
with infinite care and funfull delight.
You peopled her with creatures
huge, small, minuscule.
You fashioned man and woman
as tenants of your land,
as stewards of this planet.
O, for Lady Wisdom
that she might walk with us
and show us your glory! Amen.

344 Thursday of the Seventh Week of the Year

Sir 5:1-8; Jas 5:1-6; Mark 9:41-50

Breathes there the man, with soul so dead . . .
Boundless his wealth as wish can claim;
Despite those titles, power, and pelf,
The wretch, concentered all in self,
Living, shall forfeit fair renown,
And, doubly dying, shall go down
To the vile dust, from whence he sprung,
Unwept, unhonored, and unsung.
(W. Scott, *The Lay of the Last Minstrel*)

Madre antigua y atroz de la incestuosa guerra,
Borrado sea tu nombre de la faz de la tierra.
(Jorge Luis Borges, "El Hambre," *Los Derechos*, 456)

Our first two readings breathe the spirit of liberation theology. This discipline tries to interpret the Christian message from the point of view of the suffering and the indigent; it is a critique of society, especially where there is a great gulf between rich and poor. It is also a critique of the Church, calling her back to Jesus' activity for the afflicted and to an appreciation of the human dignity of all her members. It is not the *possession* of wealth which is the stumbling block, but the use of wealth, the denial of human rights to the poverty stricken and, very often, cruel and unjust treatment of the poor and those who work for them. As one example we may take the fact that between 1964 and 1978 in Latin America forty-one priests were murdered, eleven "disappeared," about four hundred and eighty-five were arrested, forty-six endured torture and two hundred and fifty-three were exiled. Bishop Enrique Angelelli was also murdered.[9] In 1976, the bishops of Guatemala pointed out that the individual peasant is worth more than large plantation estates, "indeed worth more than all the plantations and businesses in Guatemala" (113). How many landowners have given their workers a glass of uncontaminated water in the name of Christ?

Intercessions

For the parents and friends of the "disappeared";
For the conscience of the church.

Prayer

Liberating God of the Exodus,
the shrill cry of your afflicted
ascends like clouds of pungent incense
before your Mercy
even today.
Bodies shot through with electric power,
bodies raped by brutal soldiery,
bodies without water, bread or cleanliness,
heaped bodies,
solitary bodies,
children's bodies,
embryo bodies.
Grant rest to their souls and mercy to us. Amen.

---

[9]P. Berryman, *Liberation Theology* (Philadelphia: Temple University Press, 1987) 100–101.

345 Friday of the Seventh Week of the Year

Sir 6:5-17; Jas 5:9-12; Mark 10:1-12

. . . all (the churches) regard divorce as something like cutting up a living body, as a kind of surgical operation. Some of them think the operation so violent that it cannot be done at all; others admit it as a desperate remedy in extreme cases. They are all agreed that it is more like having both your legs cut off than it is like dissolving a business partnership or even deserting a regiment. What they all disagree with is the modern view that it is a simple readjustment of partners, to be made whenever people feel they are no longer in love with one another or when either of them falls in love with someone else.

(C. S. Lewis, *Mere Christianity*)

*Hoy he sentido el río entero
en mis brazos . . . Lo he sentido
en mis brazos, trémulo y vivo
como el cuerpo de un hombre verde . . . .*

(Dulce Maria Loynaz, "Abrazo," *Once Grandes*, 422)

Our first reading concerns friendship, and the gospel addresses the relationship between man and woman in marriage. After the loss of her daughter a friend said to me: "I have lost not only a daughter but a friend." Her words were deeply moving. Yet ideally marriage partners should also enjoy friendship with one another especially in the Western world where we no longer have arranged marriages, where a person can choose his/her partner. Yet even in the ancient world there was a desire for marital friendship. Ischomachus in Xenophon's *Oeconomicus* speaks about a man choosing "the best partner of home and children" and he continues, "For one of the blessings in which we shall share is the acquisition of the very best of allies and the very best of support in old age." Further on he alludes to a "perfect partnership in mutual service," and he claims that it was for this reason that the gods coupled female and male together. Further, the Roman orator, Cicero, asserts that "nothing is so comfortable to nature and nothing so adaptable to our fortunes whether they be favourable or adverse than friendship" (*De Amicitia* 5:17). Thus one should enter upon marriage only after extremely careful thought and divorce should occur only if there is a serious cause, certainly not to cater to the whim of a partner. Jewish tradition holds that a man without a wife is without good, help, joy, blessing, atonement, life, the Torah, moral protection and peace. It avers that he is not a complete man and that he diminishes the image and likeness of God (Montefiore, 507). There is a Jewish maxim that the very altar sheds tears when one divorces one's first wife.

Intercessions

For discernment in choosing life's partners;
For friendship within marriage.

Prayer

O our Mother the Earth, O our Father the Sky,
Your children are we, and with tired backs
We bring you gifts of love
Then weave for us a garment of brightness;
May the warp be the white light of morning,
May the weft be the red light of evening,
May the fringes be the falling rain,
May the border be the standing rainbow.
Thus weave for us a garment of brightness,
That we may walk fittingly where birds sing,
That we may walk fittingly where grass is green,
O our Mother the Earth, O our Father the Sky.

(*Song of the Sky Loom*, Native American)

346 Saturday of the Seventh Week of the Year

Sir 17:1-15; Jas 5:13-20; Mark 10:13-16

Age does not make us childish, as they say.
It only finds us true children still.   (Goethe, *Faust*)

Sell a country! Why not sell the air, the clouds and the great sea,
as well as the earth? Did not the Great Spirit make them all for
the use of his children?   (Tecumsch, *Speech to Harrison*)

Pon en mi escuela democrática el resplandor que se cernía sobre
tu corro de niños descalzos.

(Gabriela Mistral, "La Oración de la Maestra")

People have often observed that Jesus spoke about the kingdom of God belonging to children because they are receptive, innocent, without guile, without ambition, winsome and in need of parental love. However, this idea of children was probably foreign to Jesus' contemporaries. The disciples would be astonished to see Jesus' embracing and blessing children especially if they were girls. Jesus hugs them, not only as a compassionate human being but with his own Father's love. The first lesson from Sirach would seem to suggest that we can catch a glimpse of the childlike (not childish) characteristics of the first man and woman in Paradise. God is seen as the Parent-Creator, Progenitor of Humankind. S/he made them in the divine image, which as Skehan and di Lella state, comprises "the charter statement of human dignity and equality of all men, women, and children in the sight of God" (*Sirach*, 282). God also gave them stewardship over the rest of creation, which constituted a share in the divine sovereignty. S/he endowed them with senses and intellectual qualities which are not always found in animals. S/he revealed his wondrous works to them, made an eternal covenant with them and permitted them to see her/his "glory," that is, the very nature of the deity: they saw her/his glory and heard her/his glorious voice on Mt. Sinai. This account of creation, the third in the Hebrew Bible, is much more personal and shows a greater intimacy with God than the two descriptions in Genesis. It also shows a responsibility towards one's neighbour. In this creation account there is no suggestion of only two persons, Adam and Eve, and the word translated "man" certainly means "human being." Jesus' kingdom is the dawn of a new creation and new status for the human being.

Intercessions

> *That we might be sensible of God's voice in creation;*
>
> *That we may keep our covenant with our neighbor.*

Prayer

> *Fashioner of Our Bodies,*
> > *Breath of our Breath,*
> > > *Soul of our Soul,*
> > > > *teach us to tiptoe upon this earth.*
> *Make us sensible of your delicate web of Beauty,*
> > *woven in every plant, animal, man, woman.*
> *Gentle our fingers*
> > *lest we rend your Spirit. Amen.*

83 Eighth Sunday of the Year
Cycle A

Isa 49:14-15; 1 Cor 4:1-5; Matt 6:24-34

*. . . And so our mothers and our grandmothers have, more often
than not anonymously, handed on the creative spark, the seed of
the flower they themselves never hoped to see, or like a sealed letter they could not plainly read.*

(Alice Walker, quoted by Mary Grey: *Feminism:
Redemption and Christian Tradition*, Mystic, Connecticut:
Twenty-Third Pub., 102)

*Al llegar la medianoche
y romper en llanto el Niño,
las cien bestias despertaron
y el establo se hizo vivo.*

(Gabriela Mistral, *El Establo, Desolación*, 61)

Our first reading and the gospel complement one another by speaking of God first as Mother (Isa 49:14-15) and then as Father (Matt 6).
Both genders are, of course, inappropriate for neither can adequately
express the providence and love of God towards humankind. Yet our
century has furnished abundant proof that reflection on the feminine
aspect of God has added a great deal to our theology. Feminist theology is not without biblical roots for in the Hebrew Scriptures the Spirit
is always female, as also is Divine Wisdom (Wisdom 7). Let us contemplate this reinterpretation of a traditional psalm by Jane Morley
(*Celebrating Women*, Wilton, Connecticut: Morehouse Barlow, 1988,
155–156):

*I will praise God, my Beloved
for she is altogether lovely.*

*Her presence satisfies my soul;
she fills my sense to overflowing
so that I cannot speak.*

*Her touch brings me to life;
the warmth of her hands makes me wholly alive.*

*Her embrace nourishes me, body and spirit;
every part of my being responds to her touch.*

*The beauty of her face is more than I can bear;
in her gaze I drown . . .*

This tradition of the motherhood of God is found in Christian mystics such as Anselm of Canterbury, Bernard of Clairvaux, Julian of Norwich, and St. Birgitta of Sweden. This maturation in the concept of God has enabled many women to stay within the church.

Intercessions

For a deepening awareness of the profundity of the Trinity;

For women who are tempted to surrender their Christian faith because of patriarchy within the church.

Prayer

Gracious Giver of Every Good and Perfect Gift,
  hold us gently within your embrace.
May we draw security from your Changelessness;
  peace from your Tranquillity
and energy from your Tirelessness. Amen.

84 Eighth Sunday of the Year
Cycle B

Hos 2:16, 17, 21-22; 2 Cor 3:1-6; Mark 2:18-22

There is passion in the universe: the young stars, the whirling galaxies—the living, pulsing earth thrives in the passionate embrace of life itself. Our love for one another is the language of our passionate God. . . . It is desire that spins us round, desire that sends the blood through our veins, desire that draws us into one another's arms and onward in the lifelong search for God's face—in the touch of each other's hands we feel God's presence.
  (quoted from Sallie McFague, *Models of God, theology for an ecological, nuclear age*, Philadelphia: Fortress, 1987, 130)[10]

. . .

eres, Señor, la soledad sonora . . . .
  (Miguel de Unamuno, "El Cristo de Velázquez,"
  Antología, Onis, 223)

[10]Dr. McFague says in note six "This passage, from a play on the subject of God as lover, was submitted to my course on the models of God by Sandra Ward-Angell" (210).

The covenant bond between God and the chosen people is often expressed in nuptial terms. We find this in the first lesson for God brought the people from the slavery in Egypt and established the greatest of all covenants with them on Mount Sinai. The rabbis saw this as the Days of Espousals.

> Moses betook himself to the encampment and awakened them with these words: "Arise from your sleep, the bridegroom is at hand, and is waiting to lead his bride under the marriage-canopy." Moses, at the head of the procession, hereupon brought the nation to its bridegroom, God, to Sinai, himself going up the mountain. (Ginzberg, Legends of the Jews)

Some sources understand the Torah as the bridegroom, Israel as the bride and God or Moses as the best man. Contemporary men and women theologians are also reconsidering God as Lover. It is a natural title arising from the fact that God is love and shares that love with us. Even the nonChristian philosophers knew this for they spoke of a "romantic" love (erōs) which gives us possession of the highest good. So the word "lover" denotes one who is passionately attracted to the highest of virtues and it is not inappropriate that the emotions come into play here. This love is faithful, durable, able to face difficulties and misunderstandings. McFague (Models of God, 132) says, ". . . the testing of continued valuableness between lovers becomes acute." It is this "testing" that toughens love. God as Lover comes to us also as an Incomparable Friend.

Intercessions

> For freedom to enjoy our emotions;
> For a passionate desire to love the world and its Maker.

Prayer

> Friend, Lover, Spouse,
>   reveal to us the depth of your passion.
> May oblivion take wing,
>   may indifference dissolve like sun-touched ice
> that we might discern
>   the stroke of your love
> in every atom of the world we share. Amen.

85 Eighth Sunday of the Year
Cycle C

Sir 27:4-7; 1 Cor 15:54-58; Luke 6:39-45

We know how to speak many falsehoods which resemble real things,
but we know, when we will, how to speak true things.

(Hesiod, Theogony)

I want (lack) that glib and oily art,
To speak and purpose not. (Shakespeare, *King Lear*, 1.1.227–28)

Pido con voz de sangre por mis ojos,
con voz de madre por mis ojos vengo,
con voz crucificada en mis temores
pido, Señor, más luz: ahora espero.

(Ramón de Garciasol, Plegaria, Antología, Cano, 161)

Our first and third readings complement one another. Sirach uses three striking similes to show that one's inner dispositions are unconsciously revealed in our speech. The first simile is startling. Skehan and di Lella (Sirach, *The Anchor Bible*, 354) quote Box-Oesterley and Smend with reference to it: The wheat that "has been threshed for the first time is placed in [the sieve] and sifted; the refuse, i.e. the dung of the oxen which has been trodden into the straw, remains behind, while the grain passes through the sieve." The point of the comparison in v. 4 is that a person's faults (lit. "filth") remain behind "when he speaks," i.e. his filth becomes obvious to all who hear him. The second simile likens a person's words to a potter's vessel tested by the furnace. Thirdly, Sirach says that only a pruned and tended tree produces good fruit. The gospel reading uses a similar technique to describe purity of disposition but it places the burden of proof upon the person himself/herself. One cannot lead others unless one has the ability of self-criticism; similarly one cannot become a teacher unless one has studied industriously with one's own tutor and one cannot correct others unless one takes the "two by four" out of one's own eye. Lastly, weeds do not produce good edible fruits but only tended and pruned trees do this, again a challenge to self-examination and discipline. But there seems to be a certain "burlesque" in these sayings; perhaps Jesus spoke them with a twinkle in his eye!

Intercessions

For speech that is honest and sincere;
For the charism of brevity in speech;
For the cessation of verbal abuse.

Prayer

Creator God, you spoke
and the world shook off the rags of chaos.
With dreadful confidence,
you entrusted humankind
with the awesome gift of speech.
May we realize its power,
treasure it, gentle it, tame it.
May our words
be spoken in wisdom,
graced with gentleness,
winged with hope,
be vehicles of life.
May our speech be worthy to unite
with your Creative Word. Amen.

347 Monday of the Eighth Week of the Year

Sir 17:19-27; 1 Pet 1:3-9; Mark 10:17-27

The company of just and righteous men is better than wealth and
a rich estate.

> (Euripides, *Aegeus*, fragment 7, trans. M. H. Morgan)

Amé, fuí amado, el sol acarició mi faz.
¡Vida, nada me debes! ¡Vida, estamos en paz!

> (Amado Nervo, "En Paz," *Antología*, Onis, 408)

Our second and third readings speak of true or genuine wealth. In the moving passage from Mark, Jesus looks at the young man with love and requests him to surrender his riches if he wishes to become a disciple. He is asked to surrender his inheritance. In 1 Peter the author speaks of the "imperishable inheritance" of the kingdom and eternal life bequeathed to us by Christ. In the earlier Hebrew Scriptures, the inheritance comprised the land of Israel but in the later books God himself/herself is this very inheritance (e.g. Ps 16:5; 73:25; Dan 12:13). In the Christian Scriptures our inheritance means the fullness of everlasting life in the "festal gathering" of the saints. This privilege is consequent upon our rebirth through baptism. As children we have the status of heirs and heiresses. This inherited wealth cannot fail or diminish or become corrupt. As Wisdom 12:1 says, God's imperishable Spirit is in all things for God is the lover of souls.

But even on this earth one can inherit not only material wealth but virtues, talents, dispositions.

The Tennessee writer, Mikki Giovanni, wrote:

> I really hope no white person ever has cause
> to write about me
> because they never understand
> Black Love is Black wealth and they'll
> probably talk about my hard childhood
> and never understand that
> all the while I was quite happy.

Intercessions

> That we may not disappoint Christ like the rich young man;
>
> That we may experience the reality of our baptism and the wealth we have received.

Prayer

> God, Our Compassionate Saviour,
>   forgive our senseless and inhumane destruction
> of the riches of our world.
>   Even now assist us that
> we may recreate a new and felicitous world
>   from the one which we have wounded. Amen.

348 Tuesday of the Eighth Week of the Year

Sir 35:1-12; 1 Pet 1:10-16; Mark 10:28-31

*The setting sun is reflected from the windows of the almshouse
as brightly as from the rich man's abode.*

(Thoreau, *The Pond in Winter*)

*Se quisiera tocar todas las puertas,
y preguntar por no sé quién; y luego
ver a los pobres, y llorando quedos,
dar pedacitos de pan fresco a todos.*

(César Vallejo, "El Pan Nuestro," *Los Derechos*, 454)

The first reading states clearly that almsgiving and deeds of loving
kindness are equivalent—or, indeed, more important—than liturgical
sacrifice. Indeed, in Jewish tradition almsgiving was regarded as sacred in the deepest sense of the word. One may consider the following maxims: "He who gives alms in secret is greater than Moses" (*Baba
Bathra* 9b); "almsgiving weighs as much as all the other commandments" (*Baba Bathra* 9a); "All the almsgiving and loving deeds which
the Israelites do in this world are great advocates between them and
their Father in heaven. Great is almsgiving, for it brings the Redemption nearer" (*Baba Bathra* 10a). In the gospel, after the young man whom
Jesus asked to give up his riches had turned away, Peter declared that
the disciples had given up all to follow the Master. Indeed, the early
Palestinian charismatic group of disciples were content to be homeless, leave their families and their possessions and travel even without a staff for self-defence. They were not the only people to adopt
this manner of life in the ancient world; for example, the Cynic
philosophers were willing to live a similar, itinerant life. Epictetus, a
slave-philosopher says:

*And how is it possible for a man who has nothing, who is naked,
without home or hearth, in squalor, without a slave, without a
city, to live serenely? Behold, God has sent you the man who will
show in practice that it is possible. "Look at me," he says, "I
am without a home, without a city, without property, without
a slave; I sleep on the ground; I have neither wife nor children,
no miserable governor's mansion, but only earth, and sky, and
one rough cloak. . . . Who, when he lays eyes upon me, does not
feel that he is seeing his king and his master?"* (Epictetus)

In a similar way Jesus and his early disciples went far beyond the charity of almsgiving and surrendered all they had, just as Jesus had invited the rich young man to do.

Intercessions

> *For the gift of generosity;*
>
> *For the grace to give graciously.*

Prayer

> *God of Glory and of Meekness,*
> *Your Son set aside his Majesty*
> *and girded himself with a towel*
> *to wash the feet of his disciples.*
> *Gird us with humility and selflessness*
> *that we may follow his example. Amen.*

349   Wednesday of the Eighth Week of the Year

Sir 36:1, 5-6, 10-17; 1 Pet 1:18-25; Mark 10:32-45

> *But life is, what none can express,*
> *A quickness, which my God hath kiss'd.*
> > (Henry Vaughan, *Quickness*)

> *Y cada pueblo libertado*
> *era un hazaña del poeta y era un poema del soldado.*
> *Y fue crucificado.*
> > (Louis Lloréns Torres, "Bolívar," *Los Derechos*, 308)

Both the second and third readings address themselves to the meaning of Christ's death. They understand this to be a ransom through which Jesus rescued humankind. The word "ransom" was used in various senses: to manumit a slave; to release a prisoner; to buy back mortgaged property; to save a person from the death penalty or to redeem or buy back one's first born son, who belonged to God. Later uses of the word are associated with victory over one's enemies and deliverance from death or exile. But these words of Jesus must be seen in their context. Jesus has just repudiated James and John's request to be seated beside him when he comes into his glory. Jesus does not face glory but ignominy and for this reason he sees his destiny in a different light. Just as the Servant of the Lord in Isaiah 52 and 53 and the wise in Daniel 11:33; 12:3 justify many, not only by their teaching, but also by their death—for they are martyrs—so Jesus does the same. In Jewish belief the deaths of martyrs atone and intercede for Israel. Jesus, unlike James and John in this reading, deliberately chose poverty and associated with poor and even "disreputable" persons. For this reason he was rejected by his peers. The disciples found it very difficult to understand this especially as they thought of the Son of Humanity as a supernatural figure who, according to Daniel 7:13-14 would receive homage and service from the entire cosmos. Jesus turns mundane norms upside down. The Son of Humanity came to this earth, not to receive human honour, but to serve humanity in the capacity of a slave. He also accepted the type of death penalty that was only served upon slaves.

Intercessions

For the ability to find purpose in suffering;

For our rebirth through the "living and enduring word of God."

Prayer

Jested God,
you brooked neither scorn nor pain,
you went to "calamities depths"
for your friends.
Teach us the true meaning of GLORY. Amen.

350 Thursday of the Eighth Week of the Year

Sir 42:15-25; 1 Pet 2:2-5, 9-12; Mark 10:46-52

If a man will comprehend the richness and variety of the universe, and inspire his mind with a due measure of wonder and of awe, he must contemplate the human intellect not only on its heights of genius but in its abysses of ineptitude . . . .

(trans. A. E. Houseman, *Manilius Manilii Astronomicon Liber Primus,* 2d ed. of earlier editors of Manilius, 1937)

Y miramos al cielo. Y abatimos la frente.
Y decimos: —Mañana.
(Leopoldo de Luis, "Elegía en Otoño," *Antología,* Cano, 229)

Sirach tells us that only one who is spiritually and/or physically blind can fail to see God's glory in creation. Even the angels cannot adequately praise God for its splendor. But the blind person also fails in other aspects. S/he neither recognizes God's omniscience and omnipotence nor fathoms the mysteries of the human heart nor comprehends perplexities of the abyss. God has control over chaos and he knows the past, present and future destiny of each human being.

Nevertheless, some human beings, especially artists and poets, do gain flashes of insight. In the light of this reading the gospel passage is quite overwhelming. It is the blind man who penetrates the secret of Jesus' identity, recognizes his omniscience and omnipotence and praises it in his ready response to the call of Jesus and his immediate acceptance of discipleship.

Intercessions

For the charism of artistic appreciation;
For the insight of faith.

Prayer

God of Infinite Love,
your plans exceed our most ardent hopes.
Never let us cease to experience astonished joy
THAT GOD BECOME HUMAN. Amen.

351 Friday of the Eighth Week of the Year

Sir 44:1, 9-13; 1 Pet 4:7-13; Mark 11:11-26

Of Man's first disobedience, and the fruit
Of that forbidden tree whose mortal taste
Brought death into the world, and all our woe,
With loss of Eden.   (Milton, *Paradise Lost*)

"Hombre rico en virtudes".
Un sistema económico sin MONEDA
la sociedad sin dinero que soñomos.
(Ernesto Cardenal, "Economía de Tahuantinsuyu,"
Nueva antología, 146)

In the reading from 1 Peter we find an emphasis on mutual love, hospitality, generosity and the sharing of gifts, material and spiritual. Such was the atmosphere in the early Christian house church or assembly. It forms a contrast with the gospel reading where Jesus finds the temple, not as a home of prayer for all people, but as a commercial enterprise for priestly buyers and gullible consumers. Mark has framed the "cleansing of the temple" by the story of the cursing of the fig tree and the report of the discovery next day that it had withered. It is strange to find Jesus pronouncing a curse but many scholars have seen this action as a prophetic denunciation of the authorities in Israel of which the fig tree is a symbol. In Jewish thought a barren tree is associated with the Fall and fruitful trees with the Messianic age.

> *Fruit out of season may be looked for, or expected, only by one entering upon the New Age who is hungry and righteous. Hence, if we ask—in terms wholly familiar to the tradition which nurtured Jesus—why the fig tree did not immediately produce fruit, then plainly the New Age was not beginning to dawn. But even this is not a final answer, for it is true that other trees did produce fruit, then the one approached by Jesus was wrong and furthermore was contradicting the herald and harbinger of the New Age.*
>
> (Mann, *Anchor Bible Commentary on Mark*, 441)

Intercessions

For good people who have been forgotten;
For those who are being "tried by fire."

Prayer

God of Worship
 you see into the intricacies of the human heart.
May we not bring sacred religion
 into disrepute by thoughtlessness or exuberance.
Let us not "make godliness the source of gain"
 nor religion a lust for power. Amen.

352 Saturday of the Eighth Week of the Year

Sir 51:12-20; Jude 17, 20-25; Mark 11:27-33

Wisdom is personified as a woman teacher in Proverbs and as the immanence of God in Sirach 24. In our first reading, this theme is developed and Solomon is represented as seeking Wisdom from the days of his youth and pricing her above all other priorities. However, the climax of Jewish thought on Wisdom is found in the Book of Wisdom, chapter 7. Here she is clearly seen as the feminine aspect of the deity. Twenty-one attributes (the golden number, seven multiplied by three) are predicated of her and she is described as:

> . . . an aura of the might of God
> and a pure effusion of the glory of the Almighty . . .
> the refulgence of eternal light,
> the spotless image of the power of God,
> the image of his goodness. (Wis 7:25-26)

> No te desconsueles, madre.
> En el fondo de mis ojos
> está Dios para mirarte.
>> (Ramón de Garciasol, "Diálogo de la Madre y el Hijo,"
>> Antología, Cano, 161)

Wisdom makes people friends of God and Solomon seeks to make a noble friend of Wisdom. In Jesus, all the characteristics of Wisdom become incarnate and it is Jesus who draws all men and women to himself when he is lifted up on the cross. This is the divine friendship. This is where Jesus' authority lies. As Sallie McFague says:

> If God is the friend of the world, the one committed to it, who can be trusted never to betray it, who not only likes the world but has a vision for its well-being, then we as the special part of the body—the imago dei—are invited as friends of the Friend of the world to join in that vision and work for its fulfillment.
>> (Models of God, 165)

Intercessions

> For a commitment to the discipline and discipleship of Wisdom;
> For a friendship which embraces humankind and godhood.

Prayer

God, Friend and Lover of Humankind,
  your Son prayed that we might be one,
even as You and He are One.
  Look with your smile of peace
upon all who are alienated.
  Make of them one new person
bonded in friendship, divine and human. Amen.